ROMA

Romanian Rescue

Sue Smith

Hodder & Stoughton
LONDON SYDNEY AUCKLAND

Copyright © 1997 Sue Smith

First published in Great Britain in 1997

The right of Sue Smith to be identified as the Author of
the Work has been asserted by her in accordance with the
Copyright, Designs and Patents Act 1988.

10 9 8 7 6 5 4 3 2 1

British Library Cataloguing in Publication Data
A record for this book is available from the British Library

ISBN 0 340 69408 4

Typeset by Avon Dataset Ltd, Bidford-on-Avon, Warks

Printed and bound in Great Britain by
Mackays of Chatham PLC, Chatham, Kent

Hodder and Stoughton
A division of Hodder Headline PLC
338 Euston Road
London NW1 3BH

Contents

Preface

Despised and rejected

The whiteness and the silence engulf the small form in the cot. He lies gazing with vacant brown eyes at the interminable ceiling. Rhythmically, his hand taps his head, trying in vain to create some interest from the nothingness that is his life. On the grimy floor lies his only toy, ejected and never returned to him. He clutches the bars of the cot, briefly enjoying the rough texture of the flaking paint, and then resumes his semi-comatose state, his unshaped mind blocking out the hours of loneliness and misery.

A sound jerks him into wakefulness. He struggles to sit up, overjoyed at a rare visit. Noticing the bottle in the woman's hand, he begins to whimper, and reaches through the bars of the cot for it. The bottle is thrust through and he drinks until it is empty. No words are spoken to him; the monotony of his life seems mirrored in the woman's face as she sullenly holds the bottle, waiting for her task to be completed. Rough hands grasp the soaked and stinking rags that are wound round his bottom and pull them off. He whimpers again, hating the feeling of air on his skin, wanting the security of being wrapped up, but remembering vaguely that being wrapped up always hurts him.

She leaves him lying on the wet sheet, his eyes once more fixed on the ceiling. He is nearly two years old, and his short meaningless life has been spent in the confines of the cot, rarely touched, rarely spoken to; one of Ceausescu's unloved forgotten children.

1

A conception with a difference

Mountains tipped with snow were spread out beneath us, spiking through the low cloud, their grandeur apparent even from above. Occasional wider glimpses of the earth below revealed spectacularly beautiful scenery, as the plane dropped lower on its descent path. The land seemed pure and untouched, detached from the horrors of its history and the problems of its present.

The plane finally bumped and jolted its way to a halt, and the passengers gratefully removed themselves from the cramped seats, listening with grim humour to the farewell courtesies of Air Tarom. The unwelcoming appearance of the armed guards and rough treatment by the security staff increased the feeling of unreality that had been with us since we had set off on this strange journey. We waited wearily in one queue after another, wondering what the immediate future held. How would the decisions of the next few days affect our lives, and those of our family?

We were assailed with offers of help on all sides. 'Taxi? You want taxi?' We smiled and shook our heads. Oh no, we weren't going to be green and gullible. No pushy taxi driver was going to get the better of us! We would catch a bus into Bucharest like the locals did. An hour and much haggling later, we were uncomfortably ensconced in the back of one of Bucharest's kamikaze taxis, speeding towards the capital. The locals obviously possessed some secret knowledge as to the where-abouts of airport buses. The taxi driver, apparently oblivious to the heavy traffic on the road, looked over his shoulder and offered to take us to a hotel within our limited price range. We rattled and bounced our way through Bucharest's seedy suburbs to the centre. Everywhere there were tall dreary blocks of flats, vast expanses of cracked walls in grey and mustard, hung with rusting balconies and surrounded by wastelands of mud and debris. After about twenty minutes, we screeched to a standstill in a dingy back street, where the driver waited while we paid him over the going rate and gave him chocolate for his children.

The hotel was grimy and gloomy. A single low-watt bulb cast sinister shadows over the threadbare carpet and shabby furniture. A middle-aged woman, dressed in a grubby overall, glanced up from the reception desk, saw us standing uncertainly in the middle of the room and then continued her conversation with an old porter sitting behind her. We finally managed to catch her attention, and she handed us room keys and gestured us to follow the porter. He showed us to a damp musty little box with two beds jammed into it. The loos, when we eventually found them, were unspeakable. We retreated rapidly and sat down on the grubby beds.

'This is *awful*,' I whispered. 'I bet there are cockroaches here.'

'Well, we always said we wanted our life together to be an adventure,' said Graham, trying to be positive, 'and this really is an adventure!'

I gave him a hug. 'That's true, and I'm so glad I'm in it with you, and not on my own.'

'Just imagine, though, what it would be like if we had brought the children as well,' Graham said, voicing my thoughts almost to the word. It didn't bear thinking about.

We set out to explore Bucharest and find some food. It was early evening and the city was as busy and noisy as any capital at that time, terrorised by taxi drivers and filled with hooting horns, shouting voices and the rumbling of trams. The roads and pavements were littered with enormous pot-holes and dangerous cracks which made walking and driving hazardous. There was an overwhelming smell of decaying rubbish and sewage, and a dry dust coated everything. We eventually discovered a small cafe where we managed to communicate sufficiently to obtain a tasty egg snack, bread and some wine. The entire meal for the two of us cost the equivalent of 70p. It felt good to be among 'real' Romanians, and we wandered back to the hotel, savouring the atmosphere (in more ways than one) and feeling both excited and nervous at what the next few days held in store for us.

It seemed hardly possible that we were actually there, in Romania, after so many months of heart-searching, waiting and prayer. Though the conviction that we should open our home and hearts to one of Romania's orphans had grown gradually in both of us separately, there was an actual moment when the whole idea had crystallised. We looked at each other after a particularly graphic news item on the subject of Romania, and Graham said simply, 'Shall we adopt one, then?' With four young boys already, this seemed, even to us, a mad idea, yet we couldn't forget it. The scale of the problem was such that even rescuing one child was like a drop in the ocean, but the idea kept returning to us. Rational arguments and logic couldn't rid us of the inner voice which told us to adopt one of these children. We felt impelled to try, believing that God was calling us to do it, and that if this was so he would make it possible.

We began to put bureaucratic wheels into motion, discovering almost immediately that the official ideological position in Britain was against inter-country adoption. However, this was not actual policy, and each Social Services department could use its own discretion as to whether to allow an application to adopt from Romania. North Yorkshire, while not warmly welcoming us, agreed to begin the lengthy process of assessing us as adoptive parents, and that was the last we heard for some months. Despite numerous phone calls (which began the era of the gargantuan telephone bill, destined to reach its peak the following year) we were not making progress with Social Services, although I did go on an instructive adoption training seminar.

Meanwhile, because of the church's aid involvement in Romania, we were able to make contact with some Christians over there. Rodica and Alexandru, in a town called Alba Iulia, had access to orphanages through Alexandru's work, and had actually helped with an adoption the previous year. When we managed to get through to them, though, they were not at all encouraging about our chances. The Romanian authorities were making it increasingly difficult for Westerners to adopt and for Romanians to help them.

After the Romanian revolution in 1989 and the subsequent opening up of the country, there had been a great deal of publicity about the rush of foreigners coming to adopt 'orphans'. Many Westerners, in the beginning, had merely made arrangements with individual orphanage directors and taken babies away. It is estimated that several thousand children disappeared in this manner during the first year after the revolution. The world was still reeling from the horror of the orphanages splashed across its television screens, and no one tried to monitor who was taking the children and to what. While most of the adopters were well meaning and caring, undoubtedly there were some who had malign intentions and seized the opportunity to take advantage of the vulnerable situation. Moreover, the government was very sensitive about the bad publicity the country was receiving, and started to retaliate by issuing its own version of events. Television commentators began to speak of the 'flow of our lifeblood' out of the country, and of the dangers of children being taken to be organ donors or child prostitutes. It became an offence to deal directly with Westerners concerning adoptions, and some parents and orphanage directors who did so were severely punished. The whole climate of opinion became hostile to these foreigners who were exploiting Romania's children. The irony was, of course, that many of the people really taking advantage of the situation, such as the dishonest lawyers who saw a way of making big money, continued to do so despite the crack-

4

down, because of their power and influence.

Rodica and Alexandru, who had only the best motives when they had helped an English couple the previous year, were acutely aware of the political climate and did not want to risk Alexandru's job by side-stepping the new regulations. However, they agreed to help us if they could, should we decide to continue, and stressed that we must go through the Adoption Committee. Suddenly, it seemed a matter of urgency to go as soon as possible. There was no obvious reason for this urgency – none of the required Social Services reports had been written, nor did we have an appointment with the Committee – but we knew we had to take notice of this pressing inner prompting and travel to Romania. Our first plan was that Graham would go alone, since we didn't think that we could both leave the children, but then two of our friends in the church offered to come and stay, freeing us both to go. It was an unexpected offer, and the more we considered it, the more we felt it was right.

There followed some frantic organising which included the arranging of all sorts of documents into a notarised affidavit. According to some information we had been sent by a self-help group, the Romanians insisted on seals and stamps on every document. We had to get together birth and marriage certificates, employer and bank references, our academic qualifications, personal and medical references. Graham even suggested putting in his cycling proficiency certificate for good measure! A solicitor friend helped us to draw everything up, and then, the evening before we flew, we had to drive miles into the countryside to visit a notary public at his home. He duly notarised and sealed our affidavit, and we felt ready to face Romanian bureaucracy. Little did we know what we were up against!

Simeon, aged six, Joel, five, Barnaby, three and Nathanael, one, were not really sure what was going on with all this activity. They responded to the uncertainty by becoming even more boisterous than usual, which didn't help our preparations. We decided not to tell the boys exactly what we were going to be doing in Romania, but just explained that we were going to try and help some 'sad children' there. To have said any more at this uncertain early stage would have disrupted them unnecessarily.

At last, six months after our initial decision to try and rescue a child from Romania, we were packed and ready to go out there. It was a poignant moment when the children all stood waving at the window as we set off for Heathrow at six in the morning. They looked so sweet and vulnerable in their half-awake state. Life would change significantly for them as well as us if we achieved our purpose for this journey.

And now here we were, in this seedy hotel, relieved to get up the next morning after an uncomfortable night. We left our cases in the hotel storeroom, and set off with trembling anticipation to the all-powerful *Comitatul Pentru Adoptii* – Romanian Adoption Committee – to ask whether we could adopt one of the thousands of needy children left as a legacy of Ceausescu's tyrannical policies.

Nicolae Ceausescu and his wife Elena had a grandiose vision of themselves as leaders of a powerful rich master-race. They stood on the podium in Peking, as guests of the Chinese government, and watched in delight as rank upon serried rank of citizens marched past. It was a dazzling sight, and one which they wanted to see in Romania. The means they used to achieve this obedient master-race was Communism, and they ruled by fear using a secret police force, the infamous *securitate*. Ceausescu decreed that every family should have at least five children, and made it a criminal offence to use contraception or abortion. Every month, all women, whether married or single, were supposed to undergo an examination to check that they were keeping the law. The sense of intrusion and humiliation that this caused is hard to imagine. One woman likened it to being raped every month. It made fear a constant companion. As a result of this policy, many families could not afford to feed and clothe the number of children they were forced to have, and had to abandon them. Moreover, any handicap or disability in a child was regarded as a huge stigma and shame, a failure in the master-race. So these children were put into institutions and left there, the lowest of all Romania's citizens. No one, in Romania or outside it, realised the full extent of the problem until after the revolution, when the Ceausescus were finally overthrown. Then, as orphanage doors were opened and naked children were found tied to cots, the enormity of the tragedy began to be exposed. It was against this background that we began our quest to help where we could.

We battled against the traffic in the Piata Victoriei, a large square where many wide extremely busy roads converge, trying to reach the building where the Committee was housed. We knew it would take a miracle even to be admitted there, since we didn't have an appointment. Amazingly, we were waved past the sentry box, where later in the day people similar to us were turned away, and eventually found the entrance to the Committee's offices, in the corner of a large courtyard. Climbing the creaky stairs, we could hear a loud babble of voices, some of them apparently quite angry. We peered into a small room with a scrappy piece of paper on the door saying *Sala de Atentare* (waiting-room), and were stunned by the number of people in there. It sounded like an international convention and looked like the end of a contentious football match. We sidled in, unsure as to how to make our presence known to the authorities and hoping that someone would be able to inform us. Some people looked very much at home, surrounded by newspapers, drinks and food, as if they had been there for a significant length of time. I decided that a toilet was a priority. A helpful American resident of the waiting-room directed me along a corridor, adding the warning that the water had not been running yesterday. What joy to find an acceptable toilet that still flushed!

In my absence, Graham had been chatting with the other hopefuls, and had discovered that the Committee was running in total chaos and confusion. It appeared that they were overwhelmed by the number of people trying to adopt and didn't have a system that could cope. Also, for whatever reasons – some of them justifiable – they seemed very hostile to prospective adopters. Overcoming the hurdle of an interview with them, even should we obtain one, would not be easy. The only way to get to speak to the Committee was to wait near their office door and buttonhole whoever was unfortunate enough to emerge. We joined the crowd already assembled outside this door, and waited for what seemed ages. Then the door opened, the crowd surged forward, and a young soberly dressed lady clutching a kettle dashed through, refusing to speak to anyone. She had an angry glint in her eye when she returned with the full kettle, and though a few desperate people tried to waylay her it was obviously hopeless. We began to realise why the old hands had brought their picnics and reading material.

The time passed interestingly enough as we chatted to various people and found out how they came to be in this situation. There were some dreadful horror stories about the orphanages, and about the way that the Committee worked. Everyone had their own tale, sometimes sad, sometimes dramatic, nearly always humorous. Laughter, evidently, was an outlet for the stress and emotional trauma that so many were undergoing. Occasionally, important-looking people went into the offices ('Romanian lawyers, representing adopters', we were informed by those in the know), but no one from the waiting-room was ever summoned, even though some actually had an appointment. The majority, like us, did not.

There were more and more of us milling around the door, and eventually this caused one of the members of the Committee to come out to tell us to go back to the waiting-room. Of course, she was mobbed, albeit fairly politely, by people needing to know answers to specific questions. Suddenly she was standing in front of me. I stammered out a request for an interview with the Committee, in order to adopt a child.

She looked coldly at me. 'You have an appointment?'

I shook my head, 'We didn't realise . . .'

'You must go home and make an application through your country's designated adoption agency. After this week, we are no longer dealing with the public, but only with agencies.'

She turned away, ignoring my attempt to plead further for an appointment. We went back into the waiting-room, feeling numb with the shock of her words. We were so sure we had done the right thing in coming. Surely we hadn't spent our precious time, money and emotions for nothing?

'We *can't* just give up and go home,' said Graham. 'If we believe that God brought us here, then we must trust him to make a way.'

'Y'know, if you say you'll take a handicapped child, they'll give you an appointment right away.'

We turned in surprise to a tall dark-haired girl, who told us that she had come to the Committee all the way from Canada, and for eight weeks had been trying to find a child. Apparently, she kept being given children who were either not suitable or weren't there at all.

'If you say you'll take a handicapped child, you'll be in the system,' she insisted. 'Usually, their idea of handicap is a squint or developmental delay, and if it's really bad you can always say that the child isn't suitable, and ask for another one.'

This, it seemed, was what many prospective adopters were doing. We began to feel a twinge of sympathy for the Committee. There was a somewhat chilling callousness about the Canadian's words, but we had to consider their implication.

We had always maintained that we couldn't take on the responsibility of a child with grave disabilities, because of the claims of our other children. But if this was the only way to be matched with a child? And what if 'handicap' was only a matter of deprivation and gross lack of stimulation? We were not

9

prepared to approach the Committee on false pretences, which meant that if we did agree to consider a handicapped child, we must be certain in our own minds that we were able to commit ourselves to such a course. It was a huge decision, and we both prayed about it in the ever-noisier waiting-room. By now, the assorted Europeans and North Americans had been joined by a couple from New Zealand (who had come all that way without an appointment) and some Australians.

'I think we must go forward,' said Graham slowly. He looked tired and drawn. 'Let's at least give the door a push and see if it will open.' I agreed. We had to try every avenue and trust that God would lead us to the child who was right for our family. This was indeed putting our faith to the test.

There was a sudden stirring near the doorway, as the same Committee member appeared to summon someone into the office. This was such an unusual occurrence that we were all taken off guard, and we nearly lost our chance to speak to her as she retreated hastily towards the door. However, we recovered from the surprise in time and rushed up to her before she had time to escape.

'What are you still here for?' she asked frostily, when she caught sight of me. She was an attractive young woman, with lovely dark hair and eyes, but the effect was marred by the severity of her expression. 'I told you to go away.' Inwardly trembling, I seized my chance.

'We came because we really care about the situation here. We are willing to consider a handicapped child, since that is the greatest need.'

She looked at me sceptically for a moment, and then nodded briefly. 'Your names?'

After I had given her the piece of paper listing our details, she indicated the waiting-room, now so crammed that it was beginning to resemble the Black Hole of Calcutta.

'Wait in there until you are called.'

The first hurdle was overcome. We squashed into the

waiting-room, suddenly aware that it was after lunchtime and that we were hungry and, more importantly, thirsty. The weather was much hotter than in England, and the stuffiness of the room didn't help. The hours wore on, and the occupants of the waiting-room became quite chummy. Many were child-less, wanting to offer their longing for a child to the tragically needy Romanian children. Some, like us, already had children and felt that they wanted to share their family with a child who had nothing. There was an overwhelming sense of frustration at the immense bureaucracy and apparent obduracy which was preventing well-meaning people from giving help to those who so desperately required it.

It was quite late by now, and our prospects of getting an appointment for that day seemed to be diminishing. This was especially disappointing because it was Thursday, and the Committee didn't open to the public on Fridays. So if we weren't seen today, the earliest chance would be Monday – a dreadful waste of precious time. We decided that whatever the outcome of the day, we would travel to Alba Iulia, where our contacts lived, that night. There was no point in staying in Bucharest over the weekend, and travel was very cheap. Graham set off to negotiate the city in order to buy train tickets and let Rodica know that we were coming. He also promised to bring back some food and drink. I felt quite vulnerable on my own, although nothing seemed to be happening as far as the Committee were concerned. I read a little and chatted a little. Some people had given up and gone away, hoping to initiate an adoption without the Committee's authority. We had felt very strongly that we should go through the proper channels, however frustrating that might be. There had been so many abuses of the whole situation, by people who either had wrong motives for adopting or were over-eager or too desperate and hadn't always thought through the implications of their actions. I wondered whether we would be able to keep to our principles if they were put to the test in the coming months.

The Committee spokeswoman materialised at the door again and pointed straight at me. 'You!' she proclaimed. 'Come this way.'

'What, me?' I gasped, flustered, completely thrown after all these hours of waiting. She nodded impatiently and I leapt to my feet, accompanied by encouraging remarks from those around me. Once within the hallowed portals of the office, I suddenly realised that I had left all my vital documents in the waiting-room. I rushed back for them, noting despondently that Graham had not returned. It was all down to me! But then I remembered our deep conviction that this was what God had planned, and knew that he would help me through the next challenge.

I sat down opposite a hard-faced woman who was shuffling a sheaf of telexes. The woman who had dealt with us until now sat down next to me and asked to see our documents. I presented her with the affidavit, notarised, signed and sealed. I thought it looked pretty impressive, and certainly the Committee members seemed to think so. They paused over the birth certificates and photographs of the children, and questioned whether we really wanted another child when we already had so many. I managed to convince them that we did, and that we were sincere in our intention to consider a handicapped child.

'What age would you like?' the woman behind the desk rapped out.

I hesitated, 'Probably a little younger than our youngest child, but we don't really mind. We wouldn't really want a child over two if there was a choice.'

She glanced down at the telexes. The other woman was still leafing through the affidavit. I put in a request that if at all possible we might be able to look at a child in the Alba Iulia area, since we had friends there. She shuffled the telexes again and said, 'We have a twenty-one-month-old handicapped boy in a hospital near Alba Iulia.'

'We did wonder whether it might be easier for our boys if

we were to have a girl . . .' I trailed into silence, not wanting to jeopardise my chances.

'There is a severely retarded girl in Alba Iulia itself.'

I asked for details, but she didn't have any for either child. The futures of hundreds of lives were typed on a handful of sparse telexes. I thought rapidly, knowing that the Committee gave out only one name at a time, and prayed that God would guide my decision.

'With our family commitments, we cannot take on a child with severe disabilities, so we would like to consider the little boy, please.' With these words, I was beginning a new phase in our lives and a huge leap into the unknown.

I returned to the waiting-room in a daze and sat down to wait for the President of the Committee to return and sign some authorisation documents. This would give us permission to visit the little boy. It was hard to believe that we had actually been allocated a child, particularly as time went by and nothing happened. I began to wonder whether they had changed their minds, or lost our details, or gone home. I was amazed at the total lack of matching between child and prospective adopter. In England, great emphasis is placed on the importance of obtaining as close a match as possible between adoptive parents and child. Physical appearance is taken into account, as well as both family backgrounds, interests, philosophies and academic abilities. Here, there seemed to be no information available at all about the children on the Committee's list, just a name and address.

Graham had still not returned, and I began to get a little uneasy, wondering if he was lost or hurt. I was also extremely hungry and thirsty (and needed the toilet again!). At last, an official-looking person entered with a handful of papers, from which she started to read names. I nearly missed ours, as she had the usual European problem with 'th'. 'Grame Roger Smeet', she called, and it took me a few seconds to recognise the name and go forward to collect the precious piece of paper.

With great excitement, I looked at it, skimming over the Romanian to the name: Robert Sanducan Toldea. What would he be like? Would he be healthy or desperately ill? Would he one day be part of our family? I could hardly contain myself as I emerged into the welcome sunshine and stood outside the sentry box to wait for Graham. In his absence, I had potentially produced another son for him!

It seemed an age before he appeared, and we fell into each other's arms as if we had been parted for weeks. The sentry looked disapproving, so we moved away and sat down on some nearby grass to sample the food and drink Graham had bought. No sooner had we sat down than another sentry rushed up to us, shouting and gesturing to us to get up. We made apologetic noises and walked away quickly. We swapped news, thrilled by the turn of events. Graham had discovered how to buy train tickets – no mean feat – though unfortunately his expertise had not extended to finding out whether there were sleeping compartments on the train, which travelled overnight.

It was now late afternoon, so we had an enjoyable hour or so exploring downtown Bucharest before collecting our cases from the hotel and making our way to the Gara de Nord, Bucharest's major station. Despite the fact that it was late evening, the place was tremendously busy, with vendors shouting their wares, gypsy families, in beautiful bright clothes, laden with baggage and children, people running, yelling, gesticulating and, not least, boarding and leaving trains. Over the whole area was an acrid pall of cigarette smoke and diesel, which permeated our clothes and lungs within minutes. We gazed at the huge boards listing all the trains arriving and departing that day, and tried to make sense of all the abbreviations and figures. Eventually, we worked out which platform we needed. Sure enough, when we got there a large notice listed Alba Iulia as one of the stops for the waiting train. It was very long, with about eighteen carriages and two enormous diesel engines. We clambered up the high step and found the places specified on the tickets. After the strain and excitement of the day, we were both very tired and didn't relish the prospect of trying to sleep on cramped and uncomfortable seats. But the sense of adventure was still very much with us, and the thrill of knowing that God had made a way through a virtually impassable obstacle gave us new strength.

We managed to doze a little, though some of our fellow-passengers didn't even try, maintaining lively and loud dialogues throughout the night. The only comfort was that everyone went into the corridor to smoke rather than doing so in the compartment. We jerked awake at every stop, which was perhaps just as well since the train finally reached Alba Iulia at 2 a.m. We stumbled down on to the platform, feeling dazed with lack of sleep and over-excitement.

'Graham? Sue?' A young woman with shoulder-length brown hair and a pretty freckled face appeared out of the darkness in front of us, accompanied by a pleasant-looking young man. We nodded in surprise.

'I am Rodica, and this is my husband Alexandru. It is lovely to have you in Romania.'

The hug that she gave us was one of the most welcome I have ever received. Grateful for their kindness in coming to meet us at such an unearthly hour, we followed them to Alexandru's van, supplied by the charity he worked for. We roared through the dark streets towards the home they shared with Rodica's parents and brother, too tired to take in much of our surroundings. It was so marvellous to have such a warm welcome. The instant bonding which Christians can have irrespective of language, culture and colour was immediately discernible, and as we sipped an exquisite cup of tea prior to falling into bed, we thanked the Lord that he had brought us to this safe haven.

The next day we introduced ourselves properly, and got to know our hosts a little better. Rodica and Alexandru were an attractive couple, not long married, who were trying hard to find a place of their own to live. Rodica was a dentist, and Alexandru worked for a charity which monitored aid into orphanages. We had hoped that he might yet be able to use his influence to help us, but he confirmed that, such was the continuing hostility towards those Romanians who assisted in Western adoptions, it would not be possible. However, their willingness to be involved was great, and without us even asking they rearranged their working schedules so that they could take us to visit the child whose name we had been given. When we protested that we didn't want to trouble them and would catch a bus, they insisted and began to make preparations for the journey.

It transpired that the Committee's definition of 'close' to Alba Iulia was fairly loose! Cimpeni was a rural market town high in the mountains of Transylvania, about three hours' drive away. There was only one bus, which we would have missed had we kept to our plan of going by public transport, as it left early in the morning. We all set off just before lunch, accompanied by Rodica's mother, *Domna* (Mrs) Simu, a warm-hearted gracious lady who had made us very welcome in her home. Petite, with grey hair and a smiling face, she conveyed her care and concern for us without ever speaking a word of English.

It was extraordinary to think that as little as two years ago these people could have been arrested for showing us hospitality like this. While Ceausescu was alive, he took great pains to 'protect' the Romanian nation from the outside world. It was an offence even to talk to foreigners, let alone allow them into your home. No television or radio was permitted apart from the state-run versions, and anyone who expressed dissident views was arrested and kept without trial. Dissident views included Christian beliefs, and many fine Christians had been imprisoned for refusing to deny their faith. With the revolution came much more openness and freedom, and the Romanians were once more able to give expression to their natural warmth and hospitality.

The journey was spectacular. The mountains and forests held us enthralled with their magnificence. There was an aching beauty about the countryside which was both exciting and sad. Here was some of God's loveliest creation, yet it served as a backdrop to the distortions of man's inhumanity to man. This dichotomy came into sharp relief when the winding road rounded another twist and we encountered the town of Zlatna. The impact on us was almost physical. Out of the yellow-grey mist which shrouded the town loomed ugly black factories, wreathed with massive writhing pipes. Smoke belched out of a myriad chimneys, and the choking smell of it filled the van, despite the closed windows. Within yards of the heavy industry rose bleak blocks of flats, with more traditional houses cowering in the shadow of the chimneys. The contrast with the surrounding beauty was stark and shocking, tangible evidence of Ceausescu's industrialisation policy; a policy which had constructed shoddy factories and engineering works at the expense of the rich agricultural resources of the country, and razed villages to the ground to force workers to live in the towns.

We were glad to leave Zlatna behind and continue into the ever more mountainous and unspoiled countryside. By the time we were approaching the outskirts of Cimpeni it was raining quite heavily, which didn't improve our initial gloomy impression of the town. Alexandru skilfully negotiated most of the pot-holes which were strewn across the unmetalled roads, though we did lunge into a few of the more enormous ones. The hospital was at the top of a hill, a surprisingly modern building in this essentially traditional market town. We drew up outside, and got out stiffly after the bumpy ride. I clutched the authorisation paper, feeling incredibly nervous, and was assailed by fears. What if they wouldn't let us in? What if the child was severely disabled? What if another couple had already adopted him? My thoughts were in turmoil, but I calmed down as we walked towards the entrance, having said *la revedere* – goodbye – to Domna Simu. She had decided not to come in with us, and instead set off down the hill towards the town centre.

Inside, the hospital was silent and apparently deserted. We climbed three floors to the children's ward without meeting anyone at all. My nervousness increased. It seemed such a bizarre situation. On the third floor it was still unnaturally silent. We stood in a broad dim corridor with several doors leading off it, while Rodica went in search of someone who could help us. She returned quite quickly with a severe-looking woman, wearing a tunic dress with an overall on top. She was quite plump with a square face and mousy hair pulled back into a tight bun. She didn't smile at us, but merely glanced at our paper and then motioned us to follow her into one of the side rooms. This was the moment of truth! As we walked through the doorway, a small boy in one of the cots looked round, smiled spontaneously as if in greeting and shuffled across the cot towards us. This, the nurse informed us, was Robert Sanducan Toldea.

2

Maternal instincts

Robert was very pale with black hair and beautiful dark brown eyes which had sunk into his skull. His head looked too big for his thin body, and the bones in his hands and feet protruded through the skin in angular points. He was wearing a shabby pyjama top and had some sort of linen wound round his tummy. We all converged on him, making a fuss of him with excited exclamations. He cowered back, unused to such attention, and began to whimper.

I picked him up, oblivious of his wet and smelly state, and was shocked at how light he was and his evident fear at being handled. He went rigid, and pointed back to his cot, whining a strange, almost animal sound. I wanted to weep and weep at the damage done to this tiny being, but instead murmured comforting words and put him back in his cot. He tapped his head with his fingers incessantly, while his big eyes gazed round, trying to make sense of this strange situation. It was obvious that he was not used to being touched or spoken to. We gave him some of the toys we had brought with us, and were encouraged by the interest he showed in them. There was an alertness about him, despite the head-tapping, which gave us hope. At this point, another nurse, much younger and slimmer, came in and started to change Robert's nappy – if you could call the rags round him a nappy. He didn't like it, but even his protest was feeble, as if he knew it was hopeless. I glanced at his lower half, and was relieved to see that everything seemed to be in order. Surprisingly, there were no signs of soreness or nappy rash.

While the nurse was busy, we had a chance to look more closely round the room. There were six cots in a fairly small area, but only one other was occupied. A young baby lay there without moving, showing no interest in the bustle around him. I stroked his cheek, and was rewarded with a gorgeous smile, which lit up his eyes. I almost choked with emotion at the tragedy of his situation. The walls were completely plain, a grimy white, splashed here and there with dark stains. There was mould on the ceiling, and the pipes to the filthy washbasin were flaking with rust. Over the windows hung some grubby net curtains, so that there was absolutely nothing to look at, either in or out of the room.

Gently, Graham picked Robert up again, while Rodica and Alexandru chatted to the nurse, trying to find out more of his history. He was still very unhappy at being held, but we persisted, talking to him all the time, and gradually he relaxed a little, responding to the warmth he received. Graham rested him on the floor, to see if his legs would bear weight, but they just folded up under him, and he sat down. He really hated being out of the cot, and was afraid of the different perspective from the floor. We put him back and played with him in the cot, taking several photographs. He was extremely interested in the camera, and kept grabbing the case and examining it, all the while tapping his head. Every now and then, his eyes went completely blank, and he just sat there vacantly. It was such a sad sight.

Rodica reported that the nurse did not know a great deal about Robert, beyond that he had been abandoned in the hospital at about three weeks old and had been there ever since. He was said to be brain-damaged, but the nurse did not know any details. There was no doctor or senior nurse to give us any more information, so our decision whether to proceed or not would have to be taken on our own assessment and on what we believed God was saying to us. We both felt that there were hopeful signs in that Robert was able to make eye contact, responded to stimuli and had good finger manipulation. Yet we had no medical knowledge to back us up. How could we, a teacher and an accountant, make the necessary evaluation to inform our decision? We couldn't, and realised that we would have to rely totally on God and not at all on our own understanding. It was one of those defining, difficult moments in our Christian life. We had to be so sure that we had heard God, yet how could we ever be that sure? But after all, wasn't this the very type of child who had so moved us in the beginning? Despite the evident problems that he had and the many unknowns in his past and his future, we had both experienced a bonding with this child, and we both believed that he was the one God wanted to bring into our family.

We looked at each other in silence, appalled by the enormity of the decision and very grateful that we were both there to make it. If we had kept to our original plan for only one of us to come to Romania, it would have been an almost impossible situation. We both needed to be there to 'conceive' this new child, and God had made sure that we were. The nurse looked expectantly at us, obviously awaiting our next move.

'Shall we go ahead, then?' Graham asked me. I nodded, silenced by the emotion of the moment. Rodica spoke again to the nurse, who replied with some force. She did not seem very friendly or helpful. Rodica turned to us.

'She says that the hospital will not even consider continuing with the adoption until you have the consent of the mother.'

'But I thought that the consent was already obtained when the child's name was put on the Committee's register!' That's what we had been told, anyway. It was the first of many occasions when reality and theory just didn't match up at all.

'Does she know who and where the mother is?' asked Graham, ever practical. Grudgingly, the woman agreed to go and find out.

We remained in the room, playing with Robert and the other baby. The nurse returned and spoke rapidly to Rodica.

'She says that the mother's name is Emilia Toldea and they think she may live in a small community called Horea. But she is also known to stay in Abrud sometimes.' Abrud was a fairly large town near by. We had come through it on our way to Cimpeni. It would be very difficult to track someone down there. Rodica and Alexandru thanked the nurse and led the way out of the room. I gave a last hug and kiss to Robert and left, almost in tears. I looked back to see him staring at one of the toys we had brought. He didn't seem to notice that we had gone.

We stood in the corridor, discussing what we should do next. At that moment, a tall grim-faced man in a white coat strode round a corner towards us and spoke sharply. Rodica and Alexandru launched into what seemed to be an explanation, and the doctor replied in a clearly hostile manner. Turning towards us, he snapped, 'Get mother's agreement. We do not deal with you otherwise.' Ignoring Alexandru's attempt to say something further, he strode off again, leaving us feeling rather discouraged. We had so hoped that the hospital staff would be helpful and co-operative. Surely they also wanted to give this little boy the chance of a new life?

We stood outside the hospital, the soft drizzle dripping off our hair. Events seemed to be out of our control.

'What are we going to do?' I asked, not knowing what else to say.

'I suppose it depends whether Rodica and Alexandru are willing to risk a wild-goose chase looking for Robert's mother,' replied Graham. 'I mean, I feel awful asking them to do even more than they've already done, but we can't give up now, not without at least trying to find her.' I agreed. We had achieved so much by actually finding Robert. Now it seemed that it was all going to be snatched away again. Was this going to be the shape of things to come, with some small progress being made only to be cancelled out within a short space of time? For now, though, we had one immediate problem, and that was how to find Emilia Toldea.

Just then we spotted Domna Simu, for whom we had been

waiting, picking her way round the pot-holes and puddles towards us. She was smiling broadly, and didn't seem to notice our downcast faces. She went into voluble explanations, gesturing down the road in an urgent manner. Not for the first and definitely not for the last time, I wished that I could speak and understand Romanian. Rodica turned to us.

'My mother says she has found someone who can help us,' she said, 'a leader in the community, and also a Christian in the Baptist church here.'

Domna Simu was smiling and nodding eagerly at us, and we smiled back, wondering how this mysterious person could possibly help. We followed the others along the dismal street, jumping out of the way as horse-drawn carts rumbled dangerously near. Domna Simu suddenly disappeared through a gateway, and we followed her into a tiny courtyard, almost Mediterranean in design. The door on the other side of the courtyard had already opened, and a small weather-beaten old man, his face beaming with delight, was advancing to welcome us. He shook our hands warmly and ushered us into his house.

The room we entered was tiny and absolutely brimming with all of the family's worldly goods. We sat on the bed, which was covered in an exquisitely designed bedspread, and gazed in awe at our surroundings, while our host engaged in rapid and expressive conversation with Rodica and Alexandru. In one corner of the room, next to a huge pipe stove, was a spinning wheel with some work attached. Near the window was a sink, a wooden table and a large dresser, piled high with an assortment of pots, pans, vegetables and clothes. The flagged stone floor was covered with bright rag rugs. I guessed that this was the only living-room in the cottage. I felt as if I had entered another world.

The door opened and a small lady came in, carrying a pot of water, which she poured into a pan on the stove. She spoke excitedly to us, smiling all the while, and we smiled back, trying out our Romanian for 'hello' and 'thank you'. She was wearing a long skirt of tweed material, a brightly coloured shawl and headscarf, and thick but ancient boots. From the dresser she drew an array of cakes and bread, which she proceeded to press on us. I accepted an interesting-looking cake and ate it with sounds of appreciation. For all the traumas and fears that the Romanian people have undergone, they are still a warm and hospitable people, always giving of their best to their guests.

Suddenly, everyone got up and began to make moves to the door, still talking. Following suit, we looked enquiringly at Rodica.

'This brother, *Domnul* (Mr) Mihets, knows the people at Horea,' she explained. 'He will come with us to see if we can find the mother.'

'That's very kind of him,' I said, smiling at the old man, who was putting on a woollen hat. 'Is it very far to this place?'

She shrugged. 'About an hour's drive, perhaps, to the west.' We had come from the south-east, which meant that Horea was in the opposite direction from Alba Iulia. Graham and I looked horrified. What if this Emilia was not there – a strong possibility, since it had only been given as a vague suggestion? We would have wasted everyone's time, energy and fuel for nothing.

'I still say we give it a try,' whispered Graham. 'If it really is what God wants, then we'll find her.' I wondered if he was as confident as he sounded. I felt very daunted by the prospect of meeting Robert's mother, yet equally nervous that we would travel all that way and not find her at all.

We set off in the van, with our guide squashed in the front with Rodica and Alexandru, still talking excitedly. He was obviously enjoying this unexpected adventure. The road climbed steadily into the mountains, giving us yet more wonderful views. Every so often, we would pass through a small collection of houses and cottages, each with pigs and hens and a corn stook in the back yard. At one of these hamlets, the minibus drew to a halt and Domna Simu got out. She went into what appeared to be an ordinary cottage and emerged some minutes later with some large round loaves of bread. Evidently the village baker didn't feel the need to advertise his where-abouts! The bread was still warm, and delicious. We munched on broken-off wedges and gazed out at the spectacular scenery. Here we were, people from different parts of the world who couldn't even communicate properly, yet joined together in our faith and love of the Lord. Though we had no wine, it felt very much as if we were sharing Communion, in its truest sense, together.

The minibus slowed down as the road became a rutted track. A few wooden dwellings could be seen on the hillside, and we climbed laboriously towards them.

'That is Commune Horea,' Alexandru said, pointing. My stomach lurched with nerves. We were nearly there! Would we find Emilia, and if so, how would she react? It was with trepidation that we got out of the van and looked around. Already, a small crowd was beginning to gather. The vehicle was not exactly inconspicuous, and it felt as if the whole village was turning out to discover what we were doing there.

Alexandru spoke to the nearest spectator, asking if Emilia was in the commune. To our joy, he jerked his head further up the track and muttered something in reply.

'Yes, she is living here,' confirmed Alexandru, 'though he says she may have gone to the town today. We'll walk up and find out.'

Under the solemn gaze of about fifty people, we walked up the track towards some more homes. They looked little more than wooden shacks, perched precariously on the hillside, with ramshackle balconies and shutters. The onlookers shuffled up behind us, keeping at a distance. Diffidently, we approached one of the shacks and stopped. Domnul Mihets made his way up the steps and called out Emilia's name. There was a seemingly endless pause, while we all stood frozen to the spot in anticipation, and then the door opened and a young woman appeared.

She didn't smile, and her dark brown eyes held an enigmatic expression. She was small and rounded, with shapeless clothes. Her brown hair was long and unkempt, but the face it framed had the potential to be very attractive. She stared at us, not registering any emotion at seeing all these strangers on her doorstep. A little girl, about a year old, crawled out to see what was going on. The woman glanced down at her, spoke sharply and then looked back at us. Alexandru, Rodica and Domnul Mihets all moved forward to speak to her. We hung back, not wanting to jeopardise these first crucial moments.

The talk veered back and forth as explanations were given and questions asked. Emilia did not seem to be giving much away. She had a low voice, and spoke in a mutter, unlike everyone else, who gave vent to much expression and gesturing to make their points. I gazed at the woman who had given birth to little Robert, wondering how she could have given him up. 'Lord, let her say yes to the adoption,' I prayed. Just then, Alexandru shook his head decisively, and started to speak in an angry tone. Startled, we looked from one to the other, trying to work out what was going on. From among the crowd of villagers, which had grown considerably by this time, came a tall, very swarthy man with an unpleasant expression on his face. He shouted at Emilia, and she looked round nervously. Silence fell as the man came up the steps to Emilia and started speaking forcefully to her. She reverted to her original sullenness, and nodded at intervals. Alexandru interjected with some sort of question. It was so frustrating not being able to understand. We were powerless in a situation which could dictate our future. Emilia replied to Alexandru and came down the steps.

'We're going to sit in the van to talk to her,' whispered Rodica. 'It's too difficult to speak of such delicate matters here.' What an understatement! We trooped back to the van, and Emilia, a little uncertainly, climbed in. The crowd of spectators, including the angry man, surrounded the vehicle. I began to feel a bit frightened. If these people objected to us and turned nasty, we wouldn't stand much of a chance. But my alarmist thoughts were brought to heel by the conversation, now being translated for us, which had taken a very negative tone.

'This woman does not want Robert as her child, though she disagrees that he is handicapped. She will let you adopt him, but you must pay her.'

We looked at each other, aghast. This was the dilemma we had always feared we might face. We knew that many Westerners coming to Romania to adopt had paid vast amounts of money, usually to crooked lawyers. In Bucharest especially, there was a huge network of lawyers who were in on the sale of children, some of whom even persuaded women to get pregnant just so that they could sell the babies. For a fee, the lawyer would link the prospective adopter with a child, often bribing the orphanage director and the court officials as well as paying the mother. In this way, the Adoption Committee was by-passed, although some lawyers were able to use their influence there as well. We abhorred the practice, which was both illegal and immoral. While most children did go to good homes, there were some proven cases of children going to paedophiles or to unsuitable homes where they were abused, neglected or sometimes re-abandoned.

As Christians, we wanted to follow God's ways, and had always said that we would not buy a child from its mother. Yet now, when we had met Robert and wanted so much to rescue him from his tragic life, it was almost irresistible to give in to Emilia's demands. She obviously had urgent need of money. Surely we had a moral duty to help her materially? Could it not be seen as 'redeeming' Robert; paying a ransom for him? Our thoughts and emotions were in utter turmoil. I turned to Rodica.

'Doesn't she know that it is against the law to demand payment for signing the consent?'

Rodica shrugged expressively. 'She knows, but she wants the money.'

'What do you think we should do? Surely it's not right that we should pay her?'

She shrugged again. 'It is how things are done here. It is not right, no, but it is our culture. You do not understand how it works.'

She was right there, but we did understand how God works and this wasn't right in his book, no matter how we twisted the circumstances. We were learning an important lesson: don't change a decision made in peace just because you are in a crisis. We looked at each other. 'We can't do it, can we?' said Graham. Speechlessly, I shook my head. I knew that we had to do this righteously, otherwise we were stepping outside God's will and might make all sorts of mistakes with far-reaching effects.

Graham cleared his throat. 'Tell her that we would care for Robert and give him a good home. We want to adopt him but we are Christians, and cannot pay her, as that would be against God's wishes.' Rodica translated rapidly, and at the end obviously asked Emilia if she would agree to the adoption. She glanced out of the window of the van. The dark man who had been so angry before was staring in, glowering at us. She muttered something and got up.

'She has gone to discuss it with her man,' explained Alexandru. We could see them outside having what appeared to be a heated discussion. Emilia turned back to the van and stood in the doorway. '*Nu*,' she said, flatly. You didn't need to be fluent in Romanian to understand that. She walked off without a second glance, and I burst into tears.

The journey back was a silent affair, punctuated only by occasional muffled crying from me and desultory comments from the others. I couldn't believe that this was the end. We

28

had seen Robert, and everything in us cried out that he was the one that God had chosen to bring into our family. Graham put his arm round me to comfort me, but he looked as devastated as I felt.

'I can't bear to leave him there,' I sobbed into his jumper, 'So little and lost. We must get him out of there! And the worst of it is, I've got to go home tomorrow, and we haven't done anything.'

We had arranged that I should go back ahead of Graham, as we didn't want to leave the children for too long. And besides, I remembered with a groan, it was my grandmother's ninetieth birthday and I had to attend a big family party on my return to England. Normally, this would have been a pleasure, but not when I was still reeling from all the emotion and exhaustion of the past few days.

Back in Alba Iulia, Rodica and Alexandru spent a great deal of time on the phone, while Domna Simu ministered to us with steaming treacly coffee and wonderful food. It seemed that they knew a lawyer who had helped them last year. He was a man of integrity (apparently rare among Romanian lawyers), and they hoped that he might take an interest in this case. Rodica eventually came into the room looking amazed. We weren't sure whether her surprise was due to the content of her call, or just because she had managed to get through at all!

'He is not living in Alba any more,' she informed us. 'He has had a promotion and must practise elsewhere for a few months.'

'So where is he?' asked Alexandru.

'This is so incredible,' said Rodica. 'He is in Cimpeni. I spoke to him, and he is willing to speak to the mother on our behalf on Monday.' Graham and I grabbed each other's hands in excitement. It seemed that there was still a chance, however tiny. The door had not closed completely, after all.

I was looking forward to seeing the children again, but I really didn't want to leave Romania at this point. We had experienced so much, at such an intensity, that it would be hard to return to normal life again. I was nervous about making the journey on my own, too, especially as I disliked flying. Nevertheless, Sunday saw me saying goodbye to Rodica, Alexandru and Graham at the railway station and heading back to Britain. But though my body went from train to plane to ninetieth birthday party, and finally home, my mind and my spirit kept returning to Romania and all that was taking place there.

The next morning, Graham was woken by a banging on the door. For a moment, he was unable to think where he was, alone in a strange room. Then he remembered all the events of the past few days, and the fact that he was going back to Cimpeni to meet the lawyer. Outside the door, Dorin, Rodica's brother, whispered good morning and Graham struggled up, hurrying to wash and dress in time to catch the only bus, which left at 7.00 a.m. Dorin had already gone when he emerged, and no one else seemed to be around. Graham hurried towards the bus station, noticing how many people were already up and about. Working hours were evidently much earlier (and probably longer) than in England. The bus station was busy, with people running, shouting and gesticulating as they boarded the various decrepit vehicles waiting there.

The bus to Cimpeni was old, cold and extremely crowded. Why on earth were so many people catching it, he wondered. As they trundled into the grey-cocooned town of Zlatna, his question was answered. About three-quarters of the passengers got off here, going to work in one of the lung-choking, deafening factories. No wonder everyone looked so grim and drab. This wasn't helped by the loud mournful music played over the loudspeakers. The bus bumped and rattled its way through the mountains and forests, sometimes struggling to get up the steep inclines, stopping in all the little villages to pick up people – and even the odd animal – going to the larger towns. It was fascinating to be part of this slice of Romanian life, and for a while Graham became absorbed in all that was going on around him and forgot how much hinged on the day ahead.

At last the bus arrived at Cimpeni and Graham got off, thankful to stretch his long legs. It was drizzling again as he made his way down the main street towards the hospital. On the way, he noticed the *Judecatorie*, the law courts. According to Rodica, this was where the lawyer was to be found. He was called Ion Predescu, a man of high standing in the community. He had great authority in the area, and we hoped that Emilia would listen to him in a way that she had not to us. Graham walked into the building, amazed at how busy it was. Everywhere there were groups of people in earnest conversation or animated discussion. To an accountant used to the formality and hushed atmosphere of a large company's offices, it seemed a strange way to conduct business. There were many rooms off the main lobby, presumably courtrooms and offices. Graham realised that he could waste a lot of time looking for Domnul Predescu, and decided to try again later. His first objective was to go back to the hospital and see Robert.

Unlike the previous visit, his arrival caused a minor stir, and he was soon surrounded by a group of curious but not hostile staff. Then the doctor we had spoken with turned up (his name, Graham later discovered, was Dr Florean). As he didn't speak much English and Graham spoke no Romanian, another doctor was called to interpret for them. Dr Florean seemed quite surprised to see Graham, even more so when he heard that we had been in contact with the mother and had engaged a lawyer. He said that Robert was handicapped with a congenital disorder. Graham caught the word 'hydrocephalus'. This was the first time that a name had been given to Robert's handicap, and it came as rather a shock. Neither of us are medical and Graham had no real idea what the condition was, but it sounded serious.

What if we were to adopt him, only for him to die within a short period of time? What would that do to our other children?

It was a horrible thought, and he felt quite shaken by the implications of the doctor's words. His memory stirred and brought out an image of children with grossly oversized heads. That was hydrocephalus, surely? Robert's head, while a bit flat at the back, was not unduly out of proportion to his size. Graham decided not to dwell too much on this news until he had some more information, and meanwhile to act on what he believed God was saying, which was to adopt this child. If the mother gave her consent, then he would take that as an indication to continue.

He was allowed to go up and see Robert. The little boy was sitting almost exactly as we had left him, but the toys had gone. He struggled to his feet, leaning against the side of the cot, but soon sank down into a sitting position again. No fewer than six nurses and a pharmacist converged on the ward with Graham, making a fuss of the two children there and giving them each a bottle of milk through the bars of the cot. The hospital appeared over-staffed; Graham wondered why the nurses didn't spend more time with the children, as they appeared to have nothing much else to do. He showed them photographs of the boys at home, which they enjoyed, and tried, with the pharmacist acting as interpreter, to explain a little of what we were doing in Romania.

Robert was still very frightened when he was taken out of the cot. Graham's heart ached for this neglected scrap of humanity, and he felt a renewed determination to do all that was possible to rescue him from his miserable life. He unpacked some of the clothes and toys that we had brought, and told the nurses that they were to be kept specifically for Robert. He was not convinced that they would be, and retained some for later visits. The nurses exclaimed in pleasure at the small gifts that Graham offered them, and seemed surprised to receive them, as they hadn't done him any favours.

Soon it was time for Robert's sleep, so Graham settled him down and left, intending to make another attempt to find the lawyer. As he was walking down the street, he met Domna Mihets, the lady who had been so hospitable the previous Friday. She invited him into her home again, and pressed on him a lunch of hot milk and cake. She was obviously concerned about Robert and tried to find out what was happening. Through a combination of mime and Graham's few Romanian words, they managed to exchange a fair amount of information. Thanking her warmly for the meal, Graham set off again for the courts. He loitered in the entrance and spotted someone who looked as if he might be a lawyer, talking to another man. When they had finished their conversation, Graham approached and asked if he spoke English and if he knew Domnul Predescu. The man, who was indeed a lawyer, did speak a little English, and said that he was just about to go with Ion Predescu to Horea, to speak to Emilia. In fact, Ion was waiting in his car. What amazing timing, Graham thought, aware of God's presence guiding him in the right direction at the right time. Both men got into the car and the lawyer, Nicu, introduced Graham to Ion. They were very friendly and Graham felt so relieved that they had agreed to help our cause.

The journey to Horea took nearly an hour. Before setting off, Ion called briefly at the hospital to check the facts of the case for himself. On the way, the three men chatted as best they could, finding out a little about each other's lives. Ion and Nicu were friends and colleagues from the *Baroule* of lawyers in Alba Iulia, and were practising for a few months only in Cimpeni, one of the outlying towns on the district circuit. They stayed in lodgings during the week and went home at weekends. They had nearly finished their stint in the area, and Graham was aware again of the fine timing of the Lord. So many reasons were becoming clear as to why we had felt that sense of urgency to come to Romania at this particular time.

The car laboured on up the steep hillside, finding it more difficult than the van had done two days previously. At one point, it came to a stop altogether. Ion revved the engine, but was answered by the ominous noise of wheels spinning. Nicu and Graham got out, their feet sinking immediately into thick mud, and applied their shoulders to the back of the car. Mud spattered everywhere, covering their clothes, as the car crawled slowly out of its sticky rut. Exclaiming and laughing, they brushed themselves down and wiped their feet on nearby grass. 'This is Romania!' said Nicu with a wry smile.

At length, the small commune of Horea came into view, and Graham pointed out where Emilia lived. He decided to stay in the car while the lawyers spoke to her, in case his presence impeded negotiations. The crowd began to gather again, chatting among themselves and pointing to the two lawyers. Graham prayed that Emilia would change her mind. Even though there was a question mark over the nature and seriousness of Robert's disability, he still believed it was right to go ahead with the adoption.

There was a movement in the crowd, and people started to come towards the car, with Ion, Nicu and Emilia in the middle. Graham got out, feeling a little awkward, and waited for them. Ion was smiling.

'She agree to sign papers,' he said. 'No money, but you find out about visa to work in England?' Graham's heart was racing. She had agreed to sign without payment! It was a miracle!

'I can certainly make enquiries,' he said, 'but I must say that I don't hold out much hope. Romania is not in the E.C., so work permits are very difficult to come by.' He didn't want to raise false expectations and felt it was important to deal openly with Emilia.

Ion shrugged. 'But you will enquire?'

'Oh yes, I will.' Emilia nodded, recognising the agreement if not understanding the words. Maybe her maternal feeling has been revived, thought Graham, and she wants to give this chance to her child. It was impossible to tell what she was thinking, but she did begin to relax a little and show some tentative gestures of friendship.

'She will come down to the courts tomorrow,' said Ion.

Graham had a form of consent in his bag, which we had obtained in England. 'Could she not sign this now?' he asked, fearful that she might have changed her mind again by the next day. Ion looked shocked.

'Oh no! It must be signed and sealed in front of the notary, and be stamped also. Besides, this is in English.' It was a fair point, and Graham didn't argue. He had to trust the knowledge and judgment of the lawyer, and trust the Lord to keep Emilia in the same frame of mind for the next twenty-four hours.

He had brought some toys with him, just little things like cars which were easy to carry, and he gave them to the children who were running about nearby. Their excitement at these small gifts was enormous. They crowded round, shrieking with joy, trying to grab as much as possible and then dropping to the ground to play noisily. Graham felt a lump in his throat as he watched them, and thought how children in the West would take such simple pleasures for granted. He wished he had brought more, and determined to come back soon with other playthings for them. The two lawyers had returned to the car, so, waving goodbye to the children and Emilia, Graham joined them and they drove off. He was in a daze, hardly daring to believe that another major obstacle had been overcome and hoping fervently that the next day would bring our dream a step closer.

3

Whatever the cost

The light was fading by the time they returned to Cimpeni, the red glow of sunset smudged and softened by the smoke from dozens of chimneys. The low wooden houses looked cosy and appealing in the autumn chill. Ion turned to Graham.

'You like stay with us tonight? Ready for court tomorrow?'

'That's very kind. I'd love to,' replied Graham, grateful that he didn't have to seek accommodation for himself. There was no bus at this time of the evening, and anyway he needed to be in court early the following morning.

Ion and Nicu's lodgings were the upstairs rooms of a traditional Romanian house. It was owned by an elderly couple who occupied the one downstairs room, which, as was quite common, served as bedroom, living-room, dining-room and kitchen. Graham was welcomed as a distinguished guest and was given the rarely-used spare room. He was somewhat horrified to discover that the primitive bathroom also doubled as a larder, with raw uncovered meat sitting on the window sill, right next to the toilet. 'Just as well Sue isn't here,' he thought. 'She'd have a fit!' The evening meal was an un-identifiable but delicious stew, with rich cake to follow.

Breakfast the next morning was more of a surprise. The lawyers seemed to be in no great hurry to get to work, and the three men sat chatting for some time, enjoying each other's company. Then the lady of the house came in, carrying a tray with a bottle and glasses and a plate of cheese. Ion and Nicu exclaimed in appreciation. Obviously, this was no normal breakfast but a treat to honour the guest. The drink was *tsuica*, a fiery plum brandy with an extremely high alcohol content. Graham nearly choked as he politely took his first sip, and wondered how he would get through the day with such a potent breakfast inside him. The 'cheese' was also a shock. As he cut a slice, Graham realised that it was, in fact, pure pork fat. Although possessed of a cast-iron stomach, even he felt a bit queasy at the thought. The other two were eating the delicacy quite happily and so, accepting the inevitable, he bit into his. At least, he reflected, I'm experiencing a real part of Romanian life.

Nicu waved his glass and grinned. 'Romanian workers drink this for breakfast to help long and hard days. *Noroc!*'

'*Noroc!*' the others responded, clinking glasses. It was difficult to believe that it was only 8.00 a.m.

The law courts were busy again when they arrived, but there was no sign of Emilia. Graham felt nervous, wondering whether she had changed her mind again or whether she was not able to get down to the town after all. He was due to fly home the next day, so it was imperative that the consent was given immediately. Soon, however, his fears were allayed as she appeared through the entrance, accompanied by the sullen-looking man who had such influence over her. Today they both seemed quite friendly towards Graham, attempting some sort of conversation while they waited and even sharing their food with him. They had both dressed up for the occasion and had the air of being on a day out.

After some time, Ion came across and led them into a small office, piled high with greying papers and dusty old folders. It was like a scene from *Bleak House*. The notary typed out various forms on an ancient typewriter of huge proportions and laid them out for Emilia and Graham to sign. Once more, Graham was very aware of his vulnerability in this situation. He had no idea what he was signing, and could only trust the integrity of the lawyers and do as they directed. The forms were duly signed sealed and stamped: Emilia had formally given consent for us to adopt her child, Robert Sanducan Toldea. Graham was elated by the victory. This was fantastic progress in so short a time. If Social Services could be hurried along in Britain, the adoption could be completed in a month or so.

There were, of course, things still to be done in Romania. The court required a medical report on Robert, and Emilia's birth certificate. She told them that she had been born in Zlatna, which was a relief as it was en route to Alba rather than miles in the opposite direction. Graham and Ion went back to the hospital to inform Dr Florean that the adoption was proceeding and to request a medical. Emilia came with them. Graham went to say a last goodbye to Robert, and Emilia followed him down the corridor. She stayed in the doorway as he went over to Robert's cot, and only acknowledged her child with the briefest of greetings. Graham wondered what she felt towards him, and whether she regretted what she had done. It was not too late. If she had expressed a desire to take Robert back home with her, he would not have stood in her way. But she remained silent, her face impassive as she watched him tapping his head and feeling the rough edges of the cot. She must think he's hopelessly handicapped, even though she denied it, thought Graham. And looking at the child's vacant staring eyes, he could understand why. What have we taken on, he thought, in a moment of self-doubt.

Ion and Nicu had decided to go back to Alba that evening, even though it was only Tuesday. Graham suspected this was to give him a lift back. The sun was shining brightly as they drove into the beauty that surrounded the town. The first sight of the ugly sprawl of Zlatna was as much of a shock as ever. There was some semblance of a town centre, with shops, a small market and the town hall, but it was covered in a black dust and dominated by the huge factories which surrounded it. In the middle of the town the main road came to an end, eroded into enormous pot-holes which no one had filled in. Cars skirted round them as best they could, and the road picked up again on the other side of town. The three men went into the registry office within the town hall, and after a comparatively short wait emerged with the certificate, copied by hand from the original.

Back in Alba Iulia, Graham said a warm farewell to Ion and Nicu. He had enjoyed their company, and appreciated so much the way they had put themselves out for him. Both were gentle unassuming men of high principles and intelligence, and he hoped that they might all meet again some day.

The Simu family were glad to see him back, and he spent a pleasant few hours with them before catching the overnight train to Bucharest. It was harder than he had imagined to say goodbye – he felt as if he had known them for longer than five days – but he knew that he would return soon. Rodica confided in him that she was expecting their first baby. In fact, she was surprised that he hadn't noticed, as she was nearly six months pregnant. Graham felt bad that she had travelled so far and not rested when she was in that condition, but she brushed aside his halting apologies, insisting that she had wanted to come and was glad to be involved. She did warn, however, that she would probably not be able to do much more to help in the future, although they would always be supportive of our efforts. Graham understood, and wished her well for the rest of the pregnancy. He hoped that he would return for Robert before the baby was due.

Back in the bustle and noise of the capital the next morning, Graham had a few hours to spare before he needed to be at the airport, and decided to visit the Adoption Committee and let them know what we had achieved. What a contrast to six days earlier! The waiting-room was empty, and only the clatter of typewriters indicated that anyone was there at all. Graham remembered one of the Committee staff saying that last week was the final week that they would deal with the public. Without knowing it, we had arrived on the very last day possible to be allocated a child. If we had left it even a few days later, it would have been too late.

Graham spoke with one of the staff, and she made a note of our intention to proceed with the adoption and our success in gaining the consent of the mother. The name of Robert's father was not on the birth certificate, so we did not have to obtain his consent as well. The lady wished him well, and Graham left for the airport with a sense of thankfulness. Many people had spent weeks in Romania trying to achieve what we had done in five days, and he was excited at how obstacles had been removed. He felt that he had witnessed miracles that week.

The children were interested in what we had been doing in Romania, and asked lots of questions. We had discussed how to introduce the idea of adoption to them, wanting it to be something they would 'own' themselves, not just have imposed on them. Having a little brother from such a deprived background would be very different from having a new baby in the family. They needed to welcome the idea themselves. We had a family holiday in Cornwall soon after Graham returned, and while there we deliberately introduced the subject of the orphanages into the conversation. We described, though not in graphic detail, how children lived there, and talked about one little boy in particular, Robert, who was very sad because he had to spend all his time in a cot. Their eyes grew round with wonderment. They couldn't conceive of such non-existence.

'What about his mummy?' asked Joel. 'Why doesn't she look after him and play with him?'

'I don't know why, but she doesn't,' I replied. 'He's got no one to love him or care for him.'

'We could!' said Simeon. 'We could take him out of his cot and look after him!' The other boys chorused their agreement.

'What, you mean have him as part of our family?' asked Graham. 'Would you want another brother? It would make it even busier and noisier in our house. And he might be very sad and difficult for a long time.'

'We want him to stop being sad,' said Simeon. 'We've got lots of toys and clothes and love to share with him.' I was deeply moved. Here was confirmation that our children would welcome the adoption. They all seemed enthusiastic at the thought of an addition to the family. We were aware that the reality would not always be as attractive as the theory, but felt that there was a good foundation from which to work.

Over the summer, there was an ominous lack of communication from Romania. Despite several letters and failed phone calls, we heard nothing more about Robert or the adoption. Ion did not reply to our letters, so we had no way of knowing if the medical had been done. More ominous still, through the grapevine of adopters and prospective adopters came rumours of a change in the law. No one knew exactly what the change was, nor when it would be implemented, but there was a consensus that it would mean a tightening up of the regulations concerning foreign adoptions. My thoughts went constantly to the lonely figure immobile in his cot, and I seethed with frustration because there seemed to be nothing we could do to get him out.

Then one day we managed to get through to Rodica. She had bad news. Ion had received instructions from the Ministry of Justice to cease any work concerning overseas adoptions. He was not allowed to submit our papers to court. The hospital had not performed a medical on Robert, because they too had received instructions to stop. The only ray of hope in this gloom was that the lawyer seemed to think that matters would resume in September. We asked about a change in the law, but Rodica didn't know anything definite. Desperate for some firm information, we phoned the Committee many times, always unsuccessfully. We also wrote and sent telexes, but got no reply. The Romanian Embassy in London was another potential source, but while agreeing that we had a case they were unable to help us with information or influence. It felt as if Romania had gone into a communication black-out. In some ways, we wanted to rush straight out there, but there didn't seem to be any real point if everything had been put on hold. We decided to wait until September, when, if Ion was right, the system would be operating again.

One evening, I received a phone call from my friend Carole Bailey. We had been friends since university, and she now taught near Northampton.

'I'm going to Romania for two weeks,' she announced, 'to work in an orphanage. Perhaps I can visit Robert while I'm there.' What a wonderful idea! I was tremendously excited, and started to tell Carole how thrilled I was that she was going at all and that she should think of visiting Robert. Then I paused in mid-sentence, remembering that Romania is a very large country with extremely slow roads and public transport. Carole, renowned for her somewhat eccentric sense of direction and distance, might be working at the opposite end of the country. But we established that she was going to be within reasonable distance of Cimpeni, and she promised to try and get there if she could. She would be there near Robert's birthday, and I sent her some little things for him, just in case she made it.

The thought of Carole actually seeing Robert, ascertaining that he was well and perhaps giving the adoption proceedings a push, was a wonderful encouragement. I was on tenterhooks for her return and any news she might have. When she finally phoned, her enthusiasm was almost tangible.

'I saw him!' she said. 'He's OK.' She had persuaded one of the Romanian workers to drive her to Cimpeni, and had spent quite some time with Robert. From her description, he sounded much the same as when we had been there. While acknowledging that he was in a bad way, Carole was cautiously optimistic.

'He was beginning to respond to me,' she said. 'I'm sure, over a period of time, he could make some progress.' Her words were music to our ears.

Meanwhile, galvanised into action by the fact that we had

actually been to Romania, Social Services had assigned us an independent social worker, a lovely lady called Mary who was sympathetic to our cause. Our first meeting, however, was not auspicious.

'I'm really sorry,' she said, looking quite upset, 'but I don't think you are eligible to adopt. You should never have been allowed to proceed this far, because you won't be passed by the adoption panel.' We looked at her blankly, unable to take in the significance of her words. It was a requirement of the Romanian courts that anyone wanting to adopt a Romanian child must have had a home study completed on them and have been passed by the British authorities as fit to adopt. We had anticipated that perhaps we might have problems speeding up the process of the home study, but it had not occurred to us that we might be rejected at the outset.

'But why?' I asked. 'You don't even know us yet.'

'And we have a letter in our affidavit from Social Services, saying that we are in the process of being assessed. Surely they wouldn't have written that if they thought we would have no chance of being passed?' added Graham, with more vehemence than was usual. Mary looked uncomfortable.

'I don't know why they wrote that letter,' she said. 'They shouldn't really have done so, because you have too many young children to be considered eligible. Your youngest is under two, which is too young. Have you already been linked up with a child in Romania?' We nodded, too devastated to speak. She smiled sympathetically and said, 'Well, don't give up hope. I'll ask for an initial hearing of the panel, to ascertain whether they would consider you as prospective adopters. If they agree to that, then we can proceed with the home study.'

It all sounded a long and tortuous process. My heart sank at the thought of all the uncertainty ahead. Were all these obstacles a sign that we had made a mistake in believing that God had called us to adopt Robert? And what about the nature of his disability? Although medical friends had said that it did not sound as if he had the symptoms of hydrocephalus, there was still a big question mark over it. My mind was beset by doubts. But when Graham and I talked and prayed together, and reminded each other of all that God had done so far to enable the adoption to happen, our peace about it all returned. Despite all the set-backs and the negative rumours, nothing had changed that underlying assurance that Robert was our son and would one day be part of the family here.

We decided that one of us needed to go back to Romania to discover what was happening and to try and get things moving again after the paralysis of the summer. Social Services had, after all, given Mary permission to continue with the home study, and we spent the next six weeks undergoing the gruelling scrutiny of Form F. If biological parents had to have such intense assessment before they could reproduce, the population would drop dramatically! We didn't object, though, knowing it was for the best, and actually quite enjoyed the opportunity to re-assess practically every area of our life.

Once the study was complete, we were impatient to investigate the Romanian side of the adoption. Ion had said that business should recommence in September, and we did not want to waste any time. So, on 16th September, Graham flew out to Bucharest, determined to move mountains (metaphorically, at least). The Committee was his first port of call, and there he met with a total reversal. The rumoured change in the law had indeed happened, on 17th July. Adoptions already lodged in court, awaiting a hearing, could continue. Otherwise, the committee was starting a new system of application and allocation, based on regulations as yet unformulated.

'But we were stopped from submitting our papers to court!' protested Graham. 'We were allocated a child before your Committee closed in June. We did all in our power to further the adoption procedure.' The woman shrugged and returned to some writing.

'I'm afraid we can't help you,' she said, without looking up.

Graham left in a daze, unable to believe that all we had achieved on our last visit had been annulled. Why had no one told us that we needed to get the papers into court by the end of June? One of us could have gone out and implemented that. We had asked so many people for information, and no one had given it. Now we had to battle against the new law as well as the endemic bureaucracy in Romania.

Graham decided that he would still continue with all that he had planned, and so went to the British Embassy. He wanted to submit copies of documents proving we were bona fide adopters in order to obtain an entry visa for Robert. He was admitted into the grand building, and after a short wait the vice-consul, Ms Hitchens, came to see him. She was very pessimistic.

'Frankly, I don't think you have a chance of adopting the child now,' she said, with brutal realism. 'The Romanian authorities have tightened up the whole procedure and are applying the law very strictly. If you didn't get your papers into court by the end of June, then it's too late. And we can't accept these documents until you have a file number to prove that your papers have been accepted in court.' There was nothing more to be done. He left, feeling more discouraged than ever.

His mind was in a whirl as he descended the steep steps into the Metro. Below him, a lady was struggling with a pushchair containing a frail little girl. He hurried down and picked up the pushchair, smiling at the lady as he did so. She looked surprised, but then beamed her thanks, and they carried on down the steps together. With her straight auburn hair and hazel eyes, she did not look like a typical Romanian, though the little girl had the characteristic dark eyes and hair. When they got to the bottom, Graham tried to find out, in his stumbling Romanian, which was the right platform. 'You're English!' the lady said, smiling in delight. He nodded.

'So am I!' she said. 'Well, Welsh really. I thought you might be when you helped me with the pushchair. I'm Mair Pugh, and this is Ionela.' Graham felt an instant warming to this cheerful person, and was pleased to find out that she was catching the same Metro train as him.

They chatted in a relaxed way, and Graham discovered that Mair and her husband John were aid workers, based in Bucharest. John was setting up a school of nursing in one of the city's hospitals, and the family had come to join him. They had two girls, Rebecca and Hannah, and were fostering Ionela with a view to adoption. Graham told Mair the sorry story of the change in the law and the Committee's refusal to help, and she empathised. They had had their own battles with the Committee, but were lying low for a while until they saw the results of the law change. Their greatest fear, she told him, was that the orphanage would demand Ionela's return before they had been able to adopt her. By the time Graham got out at the next stop they felt like old friends, and she had issued a warm invitation to stay with them whenever the need arose.

He walked towards the hotel to collect his luggage. It was a bright, crisp autumn morning, and he was aware again of what a beautiful city this must once have been. There was an abundance of trees lining the grand avenues, glinting golden in the sunshine, their leaves drifting down to form a vivid carpet beneath. Graham walked past a mini Arc de Triomphe and into a nearby park, enjoying the peace and beauty of the landscaped gardens. Sitting down to admire the view, he took the opportunity to read the Bible for a while. As so often happens, some words leapt out of the page at him, directly relevant to his situation and state of mind: 'For he chose us in him before the creation of the world to be holy and blameless in his sight. In love he predestined us to be adopted as his sons through Jesus Christ, in accordance with his pleasure and will' (Eph. 1:4–5).

As he considered all that Jesus had gone through to ensure our adoption as children of God, Graham felt a new determination flooding through him not to be put off by set-backs. Jesus had spared no effort, and neither should we. Countering the disappointments at the Embassy and Adoption Committee had been the 'chance' meeting with Mair and now these words in the Bible. Full of anticipation, he made his way to the station and caught his train without mishap.

Rodica and Alexandru's baby had not yet arrived but was fairly imminent. Graham offered to find somewhere else, but they insisted that they would like him to stay with them again. Rodica was well, though understandably tired, and at the stage where she couldn't wait for the baby's arrival. Alexandru asked Graham if he would like to accompany him on his visits the following day. Graham was eager to do so, and having a day in hand before he could meet Ion was able to agree.

They travelled to the nearby town of Blaj and pulled up outside an old rambling building, red-roofed and with attractive brickwork. Alexandru picked up his briefcase and gestured towards the boxes of supplies in the back of the van.

'We'll come back for those,' he said. 'I'll just see how things are going first. This is one of the better orphanages,' he added over his shoulder as they walked up to the front door together. Alexandru pushed through it without knocking or otherwise advertising their presence. Graham was at once struck by the smell, a vile mixture of excrement, stale food and vomit. There was no one around, although he could hear shouts and screams coming from somewhere. 'Lunchtime,' explained Alexandru succinctly and started up the stairs.

As they reached the landing, a boy of about eight caught sight of them and shrieked in delight, throwing himself at Alexandru. His shouts brought a crowd of other similarly aged boys, grubby, runny-nosed, their dark eyes lighting up as they saw the strangers. Graham was mobbed by enthusiastic children longing for some attention and love. He squatted down and put his arms round as many as he could, holding them tight, moved beyond words by the experience. An image flashed through his mind of his own four boys, laughing, running to greet him with a hug when he came home from work. The tragedy of the fatherless boys here hit him afresh, bringing tears to his eyes. Alexandru looked at him sympathetically and then turned away to find someone to speak to, leaving Graham to regain his composure. The visit did not last very long – the children were pulled away for an afternoon nap and Alexandru soon finished his business – but Graham knew that the memory of it would remain with him for ever. It was one of those definitive moments, when his emotional commitment to the whole project reached a new depth. It was all the more significant because he is not normally a person who expresses emotion easily, yet now his heart felt as if it might break. He knew that he would do everything in his power to rescue Robert and give him the love and security of being fathered.

Graham was impatient to get down to the business of the trip. He needed to find out whether the final few documents were ready, and whether it was possible to make an application to the court for an adoption hearing. It was good to see Ion again, and they shook hands warmly, recognising a bond between these two professionals from greatly different working situations. But Ion did not have good news. The medical had not been performed, nor, it seemed, was it likely to be. Medicals required the authority of the court, but the court wouldn't accept papers which did not include a medical report. It was a vicious circle, and there didn't seem to be a way of breaking out of it. Despite his previous optimism that everything would resume in September, Ion was reluctant to pursue the case at all, insisting that there was still a total ban on further processing of foreign adoptions. The rules were changing all the time but were kept to rigidly at every phase. Nonetheless, Ion was still sympathetic to our cause and offered to take Graham to Cimpeni the next day, when he went down there to work. Graham accepted gratefully, reflecting that at least he would have seen Robert again, even if he had achieved nothing else.

It was interesting seeing the country in a different season. The thickly forested mountains now glowed with rich golds, reds and oranges, and the hedges and fields were full of fruit and berries. There was a mellow atmosphere over the land, as people laboured to bring in the harvest and preserve food for the coming winter. Even Zlatna had a less stark aspect as they passed through, the falling leaves and autumnal sun softening its ugliness. The market was bustling when they arrived in Cimpeni. Graham wondered if Emilia was there. Despite the traumas of his last visit, he was pleased to be back, and eager to see Robert again.

He left Ion at the law courts and strode up to the hospital. Part of him was excited at the prospect of seeing the little boy again, but part of him feared what he might find. What if Robert had degenerated, succumbing to whatever disability he was said to have? Would he now have a grotesquely swollen head and be unable to sit up? Graham shook off these uncharacteristic imaginings, and thought instead of the promises he believed God had made, even this week.

As usual, there was no one about as he went through the hospital entrance. He went up to the children's ward and into the little side room.

Robert was still there, sitting almost exactly as Graham had left him, as if waiting for the next visit. His hair had been shaved, exposing the angular lines of his skull and making him look much older. But his head was the same size, and his dark eyes were perhaps slightly more alert than last time. He heaved himself up against the cot side, and smiled. Graham's throat tightened with emotion and he picked him up, hugging him tightly. Robert still felt frightened away from the security of his cot, and whimpered, pointing back to it. Graham didn't want to let go and held him, talking to him and showing him some of the toys he had brought.

One of the carers came in and recognised Graham. She smiled and pointed at Robert, nodding enthusiastically, as if to show how good he was. Then she took him from Graham and stood him on the floor, holding on to his hands. Very slowly and hesitantly, Robert took a step forward, and then another one. Graham could scarcely contain his joy. He could walk! We had wondered whether he would ever be able to. Trying not to shout in his excitement, he made a fuss of the little boy and encouraged him to carry on. But after another step, Robert had had enough and sat down on the dusty floor, moaning slightly. Then he caught sight of something lying under one of the cots, and reached forward for it. It was a shoe, far too big for him. He clutched it against his chest with evident pleasure.

Graham was delighted at the progress that Robert had made in the months since he had last seen him. He seemed to be more aware of his surroundings, and the fact that he was beginning to walk was a tremendous encouragement. He wondered whether the staff had been giving him more attention since they knew there was interest in him. He picked him up, and this time gave in to Robert's insistence to be returned to the cot. The nurse left the room, and returned some time later with a bowl of anonymous mushy food. She stirred it with the spoon, and then sat by the cot and began to feed Robert through the bars. He leaned forward a little, but the spoon sometimes missed, and anyway he was not very skilled at eating. Soon the bed and his face and clothes were spattered with food. Graham was horrified at the display. Didn't they ever take him out of the cot? He would have expected him to be taken out for his meals, but apparently not. He couldn't bear to think of the child's life, kept interminably behind bars and fed like an animal.

The nurse finished her task, laid Robert down roughly and proceeded to change the wet smelly rags which served as a nappy. She didn't change his clothes, even though the urine had soaked through to them. Then, smiling once more at Graham, she picked up the bowl and went, leaving him feeling sick inside at the casual brutality of the system. These people didn't hate Robert or have evil intentions towards him. They just didn't care, and had no perception or concern about the damage they were inflicting on him by their neglect. He cuddled Robert close, and prayed for his protection.

Another nurse came in and indicated that it was time for Robert's sleep. Graham had to meet up with Ion again anyway, so he laid the child gently in the cot and stroked his head for a while, speaking gently to him. Robert's eyelids fluttered and closed and his breathing became heavy. Graham tiptoed out of the room, glad to have left in such a peaceful manner.

He and Ion had arranged to go back to Horea, to see Emilia and tell her the result of investigations concerning work permits and visas. Graham had made enquiries, as promised, but as he had suspected the answers were negative. He wasn't looking forward to informing Emilia about this, although he couldn't imagine that she had seriously thought she could come and live permanently in Britain. The cost of getting flights for the whole family, and then accommodation, would be prohibitive. And then there was the problem of obtaining work when she and her partner were unskilled and spoke no English. He hoped that she would have realised all this and would accept the news about work visas with equanimity. Ion was ready fairly soon, and they set off once more on the hour's drive to Horea.

As previously, the whole village turned out to gaze at the strangers. No one actually came to speak to them; they just watched as Ion and Graham walked up to Emilia's cottage and knocked on the door. Emilia opened it, registering recognition but no other emotion as she looked at them. She was much plumper than at his last visit, and Graham realised with a shock that she was pregnant. Robert was only twenty-six months old, and she had another child of about fifteen months. She must be exhausted, he thought, touched with compassion for her hard life.

Emilia listened to Ion's explanations and Graham's translated interjections without comment. She didn't appear to be surprised or disappointed by what they said, but as always it was impossible to fathom what she was really thinking. Maybe, thought Graham, the arrival of another baby has changed her mind. He got out some toys and clothes that he had brought for the children, and once again there was a near-riot as they fought to get as much as possible. He had also brought some jeans as a gift for Emilia, although she would not be able to wear them for a while. She seemed pleased, and thanked him with something approaching a smile. They walked back to the car, not sure what the visit had achieved but hoping that it had been positive.

Ion dropped Graham back at Rodica and Alexandru's house that evening, and arranged that they should all meet at the law courts in Alba the next morning. Despite his earlier misgivings, he thought it worth putting our case before the Court President. The meeting would be crucial. Unusually for him, Graham was unable to get to sleep that night, thinking and praying about the morning ahead.

Next day they waited silently in the noisy hall to be summoned to the President's office. Rodica was pale and moved with difficulty. The baby would surely come very soon. Graham hoped it wouldn't choose that particular morning! At length they were told to come upstairs, and were led into a large imposing room with heavy wooden furniture.

An elderly man rose to his feet behind the desk and shook hands with everyone. Ion embarked on a long speech, explaining the circumstances and requesting that the adoption papers be lodged at the court. The President looked very grave and asked several questions. A long discussion ensued, in which Rodica and Alexandru participated. None of it was translated, so Graham had no idea what was happening and could only guess from the seriousness of everyone's expression that their case was not going well. He began to pray, realising that he was utterly powerless and that only God could change the situation.

The President called for some papers and consulted them intently for some time. Rodica whispered that they were about adoption procedure as required by the law. Never in all his life had Graham felt such a heightened sense of 'Please God, I need you to do a miracle'. The President pored over the papers, occasionally commenting on them to Ion, and then picked up the phone. Graham asked Rodica what was going on.

'The President is sympathetic to your case,' she said in a low voice. 'He wants to help, but must do it within the law. So he is looking at papers, and consulting with some senior lawyers in Bucharest.' There was a tense silence in the room as the connections were made, and then the President spoke rapidly into the phone, listened, nodded and then fired off more questions.

Suddenly the phone call was over, and the President was walking into the room next door, where the clerks worked. The others followed. Graham was bewildered. What was happening? Was the interview finished, and if so, what was the outcome? Fluent in several languages, he felt frustrated that they did not include Romanian. A clerk brought down a large book and started to write, filling in various columns and finally writing a number, which she also wrote on a separate form. Ion handed her the file of papers he was carrying and smiled triumphantly at Graham.

'The case is in the court,' he said. 'We can proceed!' Graham was dumbstruck. Rodica and Alexandru were smiling and chatting to the President, who had lost his serious demeanour. Picking up the small form, Ion said, 'This is your file number in the court. We need your social report and all the affidavit to be translated. I will give you the name of the official translator for this court.' Overwhelmed with elation, Graham waited as Ion wrote down a name and address. Remembering his recent negative experiences with the Adoption Committee and the Embassy, he also felt a deep sense of awe that God had intervened in the natural course of events. Everyone had said that it would be impossible for the adoption papers to be registered in court, but he had the number to prove them wrong!

4

In the bleak midwinter

The garden of the Simu home was a hive of activity as Graham, Rodica and Alexandru approached, laughing and chatting, eager to tell the others the good news. Domnul and Domna Simu, Dorin and another lady were busy preparing for the winter. Domna Simu and her friend were shelling quantities of beans ready to be dried and stored, while the two men were digging a large hole and lining it with hay. Into this, they explained, they would put potatoes, where they would be preserved until needed in the winter. Graham realised how much more tuned into the seasons the Romanians are than we are in the West. We have grown used to being able to obtain any food at any time of the year, and so do not need to flow with nature in the same way. Winter for us is an inconvenience rather than a potential threat to survival. Graham sat and shelled beans for a while, enjoying being part of this lovely family. Dorin was off work for a few days, and suggested taking Graham out the next day to show him a little more of the area. Graham accepted the invitation with alacrity. Once he had been to the translator, he had no more business to complete in Alba for the time being.

The translator, Daniela Smutneac, had an office in the old part of the town. Graham and Alexandru drove there in the afternoon, having phoned to make an appointment. The address was one of a series of apartment blocks lining the Boulevard Vittoriei. Pushing through the external door into the gloomy smelly entrance hall, Graham wondered if he had got the wrong place. This was evidently a residential block, not offices. However, he continued up the flight of concrete steps, with the timed light going out every few minutes and plunging him into darkness, and knocked on the door. The tall professional-looking lady who answered his knock was indeed Daniela. She invited him in, and he saw that she had adapted the small apartment into an office, with a desk, typewriter, bookshelves and a telephone. She glanced briefly at the documents Graham had brought.

'Yes, I can do this, but not this week. I have a lot of work to complete at present, and these are long documents.' The home study alone ran to eighteen pages.

'Oh, that's all right,' Graham assured her. 'As long as they are done within a couple of weeks, that should be fine.' He hoped that the medical and social reports would be ready by then, so that the adoption could be finalised. Daniela was businesslike and pleasant, and having paid her an advance for the work, he left, pleased that at last things were going so smoothly.

On his last day, Graham went with Rodica and Alexandru to the church meeting. They met in a large building which was still in the process of being built. This church belonged to the Baptist Union. Like many others, it had suffered under the Ceausescu Communist regime, when churches were supposed to be registered and effectively became puppets of the state. Those which were not licensed were liable to persecution. No one knew whom to trust, as there were often informers in the congregation. Bibles were confiscated, and the gospel outlawed as being anti-Communist – those preaching it were in danger of arrest and imprisonment. Graham tried to imagine how it would be to live in such a climate of fear and oppression. It would certainly cause everyone to examine how real and vital their relationship with God was. No place for nominal Christians in a country where to be a Christian at all was a huge risk. He thanked God afresh for the freedom we enjoy in Britain.

The church in Alba Iulia was revelling in its recent liberty. With the revolution had come a relaxing of the laws against religion, and everyone was free to worship as they chose. There had been great growth in the churches throughout Romania, as people rediscovered their spirituality – something which the authorities had tried and failed to crush out of them altogether. So many people had joined them that the church had bought a piece of land and begun to build a new meeting-place, using the voluntary labour of the congregation. The main room was packed, with people on the balcony and in an adjacent overflow room.

Graham was made very welcome by Marcel, the pastor, who had met our pastor, Dick Syms, on his aid trip to Alba Iulia. Marcel asked Graham if he would like to preach a short sermon during the service. Graham was taken aback but agreed, wondering afterwards what on earth he would say. He had plenty of time to think about it, as he couldn't follow the service at all.

One of the things that was immediately apparent was the division of the sexes. The women, many but not all wearing headscarves, sat on one side of the aisle, and the men on the other. The distinction was not as clear on the balcony, where there were more family groups. Graham also noticed that there was separation in prayer. There was a time when men prayed out loud, some singing, and then a time when some women prayed out loud. He was fascinated, and surmised that if I had been there I would not have been asked to preach!

Marcel was speaking, and indicating Graham. Suddenly, there was a burst of applause, and he realised this was his cue. He didn't speak for long, but brought greetings from the church in Britain and then spoke of the unity of them all in Christ. Marcel interpreted for him, putting in lots of expression and sometimes speaking for much longer than the words merited. Graham assumed that he was elaborating on the theme, and was quite happy with that! Many people came and shook his hand afterwards, and he felt at home despite the very different approach to worship.

After lunch, Graham hugged the Simu family goodbye, sad to be leaving them, and wished them well on the imminent arrival of the baby. Alexandru took him to the station and went to buy a ticket. There seemed to be a problem. The lady in the ticket office said that there were no tickets left to Bucharest. Graham found this information hard to believe, and his disbelief turned to utter amazement when, after arguing for a while, Alexandru slid some soap through the grille. Without another word, the lady slid back a ticket, which Alexandru then paid for.

The journey seemed to last for ever. The afternoon was warm and sunny and the passing countryside was beautiful, but the train was so crowded that the compartment soon became stiflingly hot and stuffy. Graham was glad when they finally arrived in Bucharest. He found a taxi and directed it to the Pughs' home. They were on the look-out for him and came down when they saw him arrive. Apparently it was easy to miss the entrance altogether in the warren of apartments here. He was grateful to be made so welcome. John was a quiet man with a warm smile and a dry sense of humour. He and Graham got on well immediately. Rebecca and Hannah were a little shy at first, but that soon wore off. They were used to having lots of visitors passing through, and were soon chatting to him as if they had known him for a long time.

Ionela was a tiny fragile child with a delightful elfin face framed by short dark hair. Mair had discovered her in the large orphanage of Bacau, where she had been working as a volunteer nurse the previous year. She had fallen in love with the sick little girl, whose lovely smile shone out from the filth and degradation around her. When the family came to Romania to live, they were granted permission to foster her. Ionela had progressed in leaps and bounds since she had been untied from her cot and brought into the outside world, though she was obviously still delayed in her development.

She pottered round the small apartment, picking up things

to show Graham and sitting on the odd lap as she passed by. When it came to the mealtime, however, she showed a different side to her character. As soon as she was put in her high chair, she started to cry and struggled to get out. Graham tried to distract her by talking to her and making silly faces, and this worked for a while. Mair explained that Ionela hated being fed. She still couldn't chew properly, and didn't even like the liquidised food she was given. Every mealtime was a battle, accompanied by screams, coaxings, fallen cutlery and plates, and food everywhere. Mair was at her wits' end.

This time, however, the cries did not reach a crescendo, and as everyone worked overtime to distract and entertain the young objector, Mair managed to slip spoonfuls of food into her mouth. Rebecca and Hannah were overjoyed and kept shouting encouragement as Ionela ate more and more without screaming or spitting it out. There had been times when the older girls had eaten in another room, so distressing did they find the whole procedure, but today the meal was over with no traumas. Everyone cheered, and Ionela broke into a big beaming smile.

'You're here at a significant milestone in our family life,' smiled John at Graham. 'Let's hope she keeps this up!' The incident made Graham realise again how demanding life can be once a damaged vulnerable child joins the family.

It was with a certain feeling of triumph that he entered the British Embassy the next day, on his way to the airport. He asked for Ms Hitchens, and enjoyed her look of astonishment when he told her that he now had a court number for the adoption papers.

'This is most exceptional,' she said. 'We haven't had another case like this.'

'It was all legally done,' said Graham, suddenly afraid that she would accuse him of bribing the Court President. 'The President consulted with other judges, and came to his decision based on his interpretation of the law as applied to our case.'

'I'm not suggesting for a moment that you've done anything

illegal,' she said, a little sharply, 'but I *am* surprised. However, I can now accept your papers for entry clearance, and we can request the others from Britain.' Everything was fitting into place, thought Graham, elated, as he made his way to the airport. Even the obligatory flight delay couldn't dampen his spirits, and the sight of me and the four boys waving and cheering on the platform of York station made his joy complete.

After that trip, we were buoyant with optimism for a week or two, expecting to hear at any moment that an adoption hearing was scheduled for the near future. But then problems began to appear again, undermining our optimism and returning us to that dreadful state of uncertainty.

The first obstacle that loomed was our adoption panel. The home study was complete, and was positive, but we still had to be passed as prospective adopters by North Yorkshire Social Services. We were on tenterhooks for the whole of the day of the panel, waiting to hear the outcome. If we failed, we wouldn't be eligible to continue with our adoption of Robert. Normally, prospective adopters have to be passed before they are linked with a child. But nothing to do with the Romanian experience had been normal, and the panel accepted that we had acted in good faith. After all, if we had waited we would have been too late.

Mary rang quite late in the day, sounding a little perplexed. 'It's neither good nor bad news,' she said. 'The panel was divided, and couldn't come to a decision. It's most unusual. Some people felt that your present family was too large and too young to contemplate another child of similar age, while others felt that this was a unique situation and couldn't be judged along the usual guidelines.'

'So what's going to happen now?' I said, hating the thought that this suspense was going to continue.

'The case is being sent next week to the Director of Social Services, and he will make the final decision. He's got four children,' she added, with a laugh. 'I don't know whether that's

an advantage or not!' I knew what she meant. We̶   ͘
but to wait and pray.

The week dragged by, and there was still no ᵢ.
Romania. We were not too perturbed about that, howe͘   ͘ it
would all be to no avail if we failed the panel. Besides, the
church was preparing to send out some more aid at the end of
November, and we had asked the people taking it to do some
investigations on our behalf.

At last, the day of our second panel arrived. It was
frustrating to think that we couldn't speak for ourselves. This
man was going to make a decision that affected all of our lives
without even meeting us. I thought of Robert, lying in his dirty
cot, gazing at the ceiling, oblivious to the fact that his fate
hung in the balance, depending on the decision of one person
thousands of miles away. I couldn't settle to anything, and spent
most of the day reading books to Nathanael and checking that
the phone was still in working order. When it finally rang, I
was trembling so much that I could hardly pick it up.

'Sue, you've been passed! You can go ahead!' Mary sounded
pleased and excited. I closed my eyes, overwhelmed with relief,
and listened to the details of the day. It was another victory
against the odds, and another confirmation that we were still
on the right track. I thanked Mary for all her support and hard
work, and promised to let her know how we got on.

We were encouraged and excited as we helped in the preparations for the relief trip to Romania. People in York had
responded very generously to our appeals for goods, and there
was a great deal of sorting to do. Three men were travelling
out in a large lorry, delivering aid to places where we had
already made contact, maintaining our commitment to the
people there. Dick was leading the trip and had agreed to find
out what he could about Robert while he was there. We had
been unable to make much contact for some time, because
Rodica and Alexandru were immersed in difficulties following
the birth of their baby, Andrei. He was diagnosed as having

many problems, including heart and brain damage. They had to take him to a distant town for treatment, and were in a state of great shock and distress. There was talk of Rodica and Andrei perhaps coming to England for treatment, helped by a couple who had adopted from Alba the previous year. It was our hope and prayer that this would be possible. Meanwhile we sent messages of support and did not bother them with our own problems. So it was very good timing from our point of view that the church was going out there now. We knew that Dick would do his utmost to further the adoption, and we briefed him with all the information we thought he would need.

It was over a week before they returned, and we had heard nothing in between except brief messages that they had arrived safely. They were based in Cluj, but were making journeys to other places, including Alba Iulia. We were desperate to find out what they had been able to do for us, and did not give them long to get over their travel exhaustion before going round to find out. But the news was very disturbing. Dick had been told by Alexandru that there were rumours that Robert had been moved from Cimpeni to Alba itself. He didn't know why, but presumed it was because the hospital no longer wanted to look after the child and so had transferred him to the nearest orphanage. Or was it something sinister to do with the adoption? Were they trying to hide him from us?

Dick had visited the orphanage with some aid; he had visited it before, and was shown round as an honoured guest. However, as soon as he had mentioned Robert and the fact that he knew us, it was as if a door had been slammed in his face. They hurried him out of the orphanage, refusing to give him any information about Robert and appearing quite hostile. They wouldn't even say whether Robert was there or not. Dick had not been able to make contact with Ion in the short time he had been in Romania, so we were no wiser as to what was going on. Certainly, it did not seem as if the adoption was progressing at all. Even worse, there was the distinct impression that for some reason people were actively trying to prevent it. We decided that another trip was necessary. There was a grave danger that Robert might disappear altogether into the orphanage system of Romania. We had to find him.

So it was that a week later, I was jerked from sleep by the unsympathetic shrilling of the alarm. It was half past five in the morning. Why, I wondered, as I staggered out of bed, feeling sick, did this adventure necessitate so many early starts? My sister Elizabeth, who was coming with me, was up, also looking rather bleary-eyed, and we convened at the kettle while our more lively husbands brought the cases down and checked the tickets and passports. I felt terrified at the whole prospect of going now, and wished that I was still safely snuggled up in bed, with no more arduous a trip to contemplate than the school run. However, the taxi arrived and we said our goodbyes and set off for the station and Heathrow, very excited now that the journey had actually begun. We kept discussing possible lines of approach and courses of action for the week ahead. The problem was that we had so little information – no one seemed able or willing to tell us what was going on. Secretly, I hoped that God would work a miracle out there and that in a week's time we would return to England with Robert.

Elizabeth loves flying and her enthusiasm helped to ease my dislike of the whole proceedings. We looked down as the plane lost height through the clouds, ready to land, and were amazed at the amount of snow on the ground.

'It's so beautiful,' breathed Libs, gazing at her first view of Romania. 'Good job I brought loads of warm clothes,' she added, ever practical. The view was indeed very beautiful, but as we approached the airport I was alarmed to see that it appeared to be as heavily shrouded in snow as the rest of the countryside.

'Surely we're not going to land on that?' I exclaimed, as what should have been a runway came into sight below us. It looked like a flat ski run. Dotted round the perimeter were large snow sculptures of planes. I began to wonder whether the pilot had made an error and flown to the Arctic instead. All the passengers were pressed up against the windows, remarking loudly at the snow and the lack of tarmac. The plane swiftly lost height. I closed my eyes, convinced that it would go into an uncontrollable spin on the icy packed-down snow. With a heavy bump, the plane touched down on the snowy track like some ungainly toboggan. There was a spontaneous round of applause from the passengers. One wit called out, 'Look, the stewards are hanging out the back with tablecloths to slow us down.'

Amid the laughter, we gathered our things together and prepared to disembark. An icy blast hit us as we clambered down the steps and slipped and slid our way to the airport bus. It was going to be a very cold stay.

We went through the customs barrier and into an impossibly crowded room full of people shouting and pushing. There were lots of people holding up cards with names on; anxiously I looked over the throng for my own name. Yes, there it was! The holder of the card was a short, kindly looking man with a fair beard and thinning hair, whom I recognised from Graham's descriptions as John Pugh. He was also scanning the crowds of people. Our eyes met and I waved enthusiastically. He broke into a smile and started to push his way towards us. We all introduced ourselves and then trudged towards John's car.

'I think we'll have a slow journey back,' he said. 'This latest fall of snow has made the roads treacherous, because of all the ice underneath.' He was soon proved right, as we joined a massive traffic jam where some cars had skidded and collided. No one was waiting patiently in the jam – everyone was trying to overtake it, weaving in and out of other vehicles and nearly crashing into oncoming traffic doing the same thing. John was unfazed by the chaotic conditions, and chatted away about our journey and our plans. Every now and then he swerved to avoid some particularly dangerous vehicle, and so we made our slow progress to the city centre.

John and Mair lived in an apartment on the third floor of an old house. We climbed the steps and were greeted at the door by a small painfully thin child who smiled at us but didn't say a word. She looked about three years old.

'Ionela, say hello to our visitors,' said John. Ionela smiled again and ran inside, shouting something as she went. We trooped into the small hall and turned to meet Mair, who gave us each a welcoming hug. The Pughs were used to giving hospitality to travelling aid workers, though Graham and I were the first prospective adopters they had got to know. We went into the living-room where their other two daughters, Rebecca and Hannah, were waiting a little shyly. It was lovely to be somewhere so warm and homely. We settled down with a hot drink and started to get to know each other. I loved hearing about the family's life in Romania: John's work, the girls' problems with schooling, Mair's problems with shopping (no cheese, no bacon, no crisps, no *chocolate*!), their own struggle to foster and now adopt Ionela. As the evening wore on, and after a lovely meal, we relaxed more and more in each other's company. It was late before we eventually went to bed, but the foundations of a strong friendship had been firmly laid.

The next morning, John and Rebecca volunteered to take us to the station and steer us through the complexities of the timetable and ticket systems. After an uncomfortable night sleeping with my fidgety sister I woke early, ready for the next phase of the journey. We waved goodbye to Mair, Hannah and Ionela, promising to see them again soon, and set off for the station. It was still very cold as we waited in the draughty ticket hall. The whole station was as busy as last time, and the noise and the smell reminded me so clearly of the journey Graham and I had made seven months previously. We had had such high hopes then. Surely they wouldn't come to nothing after all? My imagination started to take over: perhaps Robert had been moved somewhere else and we would never be able to find him again. Or perhaps he was seriously ill. Or even . . .

'Susan, come on, the train's this way.' Libs interrupted my depressing thoughts, and I realised that John and Rebecca had managed to buy us some tickets and were now moving towards the platform. The train was not a huge express like last time, but a smaller regional type. It looked as if it would take a very long time to get to Alba Iulia.

'This is the first one going,' said John. 'I couldn't get tickets for any other.' We thanked him, gave them both a hug and got in. As we settled down on our seats, Elizabeth leaned forward and touched the window.

'This ice is on the *inside* of the window!' she exclaimed. I instinctively touched the window as well. Sure enough, it was thick with ice. We realised, with sinking hearts, that there was no heating at all in the carriage.

Over the next eight hours, Elizabeth and I kept diving into our bags and putting on more clothes. We whiled away the time chatting to a group of men who had got on at Brasov and who spoke fairly fluent English. They were very politically aware, and the talk ranged over the economic state of the country, the government, life under Ceausescu, the revolution. One, Mihai, was a fervent monarchist, and longed for the restoration of the monarchy in Romania. He lived in Timisoara and had been involved in the uprising there. His stories of it were fascinating. We felt that we had received some valuable insight into Romanian life by the time the train drew into Vints, where we were to catch a local train to Alba. Hardly able to move for the cold and the quantities of clothes we were wearing, we said our goodbyes and climbed stiffly out on to the platform. An hour later, we were in Alba Iulia, looking round for Alexandru.

He had promised to meet us and take us to the home of a young couple in the church, where we would be staying. It was not very long since the birth of Andrei, Rodica and Alexandru's baby, and the little one was still suffering health problems, so they did not feel able to offer us hospitality. We quite understood their reasons, and wouldn't have wanted to impose on them at such a pressured time.

'There he is!' I said, relieved. 'Hey, Alexandru, over here!' Dozens of people turned at the sound of English being shouted, and I felt a bit embarrassed. But at that moment Alexandru came up to us, beaming broadly, and greeted us like old friends. We asked after Rodica and Andrei, and I found the presents we had brought for them all.

'But you will come and see us while you are here, please?' he said, as we drove off in his minibus.

It seemed that things were still not progressing well with Andrei, and that Rodica had become quite depressed. Elizabeth, who is a midwife, was able to ask all sorts of intelligent questions, and we could see that it was a relief for Alexandru to talk about the whole situation. The health service in Romania is supposedly free, but the reality is that most doctors require substantial 'presents' before they will treat a patient, even if that patient is in urgent need. Rodica and Alexandru had been forced to give far more than they could really afford in order to save Andrei's life at the beginning and to secure continuing treatment for him since. We were appalled at this dreadful system, and extremely sorry for this lovely couple who were under such strain. Alexandru shrugged philosophically when we tried to express our sympathy.

'This is how it is in Romania,' he said. I found his acceptance hard to understand, but then I was a stranger, unqualified and unwilling to pass judgment on another culture.

We had driven out of the centre of Alba and up a hill, the unmade road winding through concrete blocks of apartments, many of them only half-built. Alexandru pulled up outside a smaller complex overlooking a playing field and stopped the engine.

'Come and meet Mihaela and Adrian,' he said. Leaving our bags, we walked up the pathway and into the hall of the block of flats. It smelt of cooked cabbage. Through the door of one of the flats, I heard a man's voice shouting angrily, and up the stairs children could be heard, playing on the landing. Alexandru walked past the stairs and along a short passage to another ground-floor doorway. He rang the bell; immediately the door opened and a tall dark-haired young man stood there, smiling and gesturing us in. Behind him, looking rather nervous, was a pale slim girl with long wavy brown hair and large blue eyes. Adrian and Mihaela greeted us with a kiss on each cheek, and invited us into their kitchen.

They were obviously a little shy at meeting us, but Alexandru kept the conversation going, translating where necessary. They both spoke some English, though it was fairly limited. I began to worry that we would not have enough communication to achieve the aims of the week. However, as the evening progressed it became clear that it was going to be possible to make ourselves understood, even if it was hard work to do so. Mihaela and I both had dictionaries and referred to them constantly, with much laughter and confusion. Libs and I warmed to our hosts, who were so willing to put themselves out for us.

Mihaela and Adrian's apartment was surprisingly spacious for a young couple without children, and it was very pleasantly furnished. The kitchen was quite large, with a modern cooker and fridge, and a table and chairs at one end. There was a more formal living-room with an ornate wooden display cabinet and heavy curtains and carpet in rich dark colours. As well as the bathroom and main bedroom, there were two further rooms. One was an informal sitting-room, with a television, and the other was a sewing-room, obviously in constant use. Adrian was a tailor working for a shop in the town, but he also did some private work as well. In a country where ready-made clothes are not easily available and are extremely expensive, he was never short of work. Elizabeth and I were to sleep in the living-room, which had a bed-settee in it. We heaved our bags in there and started to sort ourselves out.

The next morning, we got up at a reasonable time to go to the law courts. We found that Adrian had already left for work and Mihaela had been up for some time. She still looked very pale; we discovered that she had been quite ill with kidney problems the previous year and was still convalescing. She was keen to come with us to meet the lawyer, and we were very grateful, as she could act as guide and interpreter for us. We all wrapped up very well for the walk into town. I put on as many layers as possible, including two pairs of gloves and snow boots, loaned by skiing friends at home.

It was a glorious crisp winter morning, with the sun glinting off the powdered whiteness and making the whole world sparkle. Even the drab apartment blocks looked attractive with their coating of snow. The cold air bit the back of our throats and brought a flush to our cheeks. Libs made a snowball and lobbed it at me before I had time to duck. Shrieking indignantly, I threw one back and a full-scale fight might have developed if we had not caught sight of Mihaela's astonished face.

'Children, *please*,' she said in her accented English, and we all burst out laughing and continued our way more sedately. It was about a mile from Mihaela's home to the centre of the town, and we enjoyed the walk.

Alba Iulia was a mixture of new mainly concrete buildings of Communist-inspired architecture and older more gracious buildings from an earlier era. The houses were attractively disordered, a higgledy-piggledy collection of low-roofed pastel buildings surrounded by vegetable plots and pigsties – no formal rows of dwellings or manicured front gardens here. The old part of the town seemed to have grown organically, rather than have been designed by a town planning committee.

The centre of Alba Iulia had grass and trees (as well as a busy main road) and was pleasant to wander through. There were shops on either side of this small park area, but they were very poorly stocked. The grocery stores had shelves and shelves of the same few home-produced goods, and other types of shop had large empty spaces in their windows, with one or two shabby items looking lonely in the middle of them. What struck me most was the number of half-built office or apartment blocks throughout the town. Mihaela told us that under Ceausescu many building projects were begun, but that they had nearly all failed through lack of funds and had just been abandoned in their half-finished state, often with cranes and other equipment left on site.

We approached the law courts nervously, not really knowing what to expect. The first thing we noticed as we pushed through the heavy doors was the enormous number of people there. Instead of the hushed atmosphere and orderly proceedings of English judiciary buildings, there was a conglomeration of shouting, running, pushing and jostling crowds round doors and notices. Every now and then, a name would be called urgently over the loudspeaker, and soon after someone would come rushing out of one room and hurry into another. The building was thick with cigarette smoke, the strong smell of it causing us to feel quite nauseous.

Mihaela stopped to ask someone where our lawyer worked, and we were pointed up the stairs. A wide balcony ran round the main hall, with offices off, and it was outside one of these that we stopped and joined a group of other people who were all waiting for someone to come out. I remembered our wait outside the Adoption Committee's offices, and wondered if all business in Romania was conducted in this way. A professional-looking lady was just about to go in; Mihaela asked her if Nicu, the lawyer, was inside. She disappeared and re-emerged a few moments later to say that he was, and that he would be coming *imediat*. This sounded hopeful, but in fact it was twenty minutes before the door opened again and a smart dark-haired man in his mid-thirties came out.

He smiled at us and shook hands, while Mihaela introduced us and reminded him of our circumstances. He had met Graham in Cimpeni, where he had been working with Ion, and was happy to take on the case now, since Ion was unable to continue. He went into voluble explanations with Mihaela, seeming very serious and almost angry. She didn't stop to translate, and we were left looking from one to the other, as at a tennis match, wondering what on earth they were saying. Eventually they stopped, and Mihaela turned to us.

'He say that adoption is very difficult now. The papers is not ready July.' It had taken him a very long time to say that, but I was at the mercy of Mihaela, who was unsure of her English.

'Yes, but the papers have been accepted at this court, so now we want to complete the process.' She looked puzzled. 'We want to find Robert and adopt him as soon as possible. The court said that we can adopt, but nothing more has been done since September when Graham was here.' I found that my voice had risen as I tried to communicate. She nodded, and translated to Nicu. He shrugged and answered briefly.

'He say OK we try,' said Mihaela.

I smiled in relief, and turned to Nicu. 'Thank you. Do you know where Robert is? We need to have a medical done on him for the adoption papers.'

Without waiting for Mihaela, he replied, 'He is in Alba, in the *Casa de Copii*.' This, I knew, meant orphanage, and my heart lifted at the knowledge that he was here in the town. He had not disappeared, and we would not have to make a three-hour bus journey every time we wanted to see him. Nicu and Mihaela were talking again, and then, with a slight bow in our direction, he said *la revedere* and went back into his office. Mihaela was consulting her dictionary again. 'We must meet him at one o'clock to go to the *casa*,' she said, 'see the director.' Libs and I looked at each other in excitement. At last we seemed to be making progress.

5

By faith, not by sight

Leagunul de Copii Nr 1 in Alba Iulia is a large white concrete building standing behind a high fence. It stretches away from the road in its own grounds, and presents a strangely blank face to the outside world. A transfer of Rupert the Bear looks out from one of the barred windows, and piles of dirty laundry adorn the balconies. It is in a residential street, just across the road, I suddenly realised, from Rodica and Alexandru's house. How curious to live so close to one of Romania's infamous orphanages, and be unaware of what is going on.

We felt very nervous as we stopped at the gate. What would we find inside? All the horror of the television images flooded back into my mind. I didn't know if I could cope with what I might see. Beside me, Libs and Mihaela both looked tense, and even Nicu, for all his authority, seemed uneasy as he pressed the bell. No one answered, so he pushed open the gate and peered through.

The place was deserted as we walked slowly along the path to the main door. A dreadful stench hit us as we walked into the building, a smell of human filth and rotting food. It was disgusting, and our faces all registered shock at this unexpected assault. Then we noticed the noise: children wailing and shouting, sobs and shrieks and almost animal grunts, the more strident tones of adults' voices raised in anger or irritation. I didn't hear any laughter. I gritted my teeth and forced myself to stay still and not run out of the door and away from the sights which would inevitably accompany the smell and the noise. Nicu, with a grim face, walked to a nearby doorway and spoke to the person in the room. I was pretty sure that he had never been in an orphanage before. He gestured us to come in and we sat down in silence to wait for the director of the orphanage. I noticed a glass display cabinet in a corner of the room. It was full of toys.

After a few moments she walked in, a hard-faced woman with cold blue eyes. She did not look pleased to see us, and merely nodded slightly when Nicu introduced us. Her name was Dr Popescu. She was, we learnt later, eminent in her profession. As the lawyer explained our purpose and showed her the document from the Committee, the severe expression on her face hardened. She snapped out a reply and then went into a longer speech, with Nicu joining in at intervals and putting a different argument. Eventually she nodded and called to an assistant.

'She does not like adoptions – make trouble with the government,' Mihaela whispered to us.

'But she can't stop us, can she?' I whispered back.

'Not if you have documents. We go see him now.'

We all stood up and followed the nurse out of the room. For some reason, she was wearing a towelling dressing-gown over her clothes. We went up the stone steps, towards the noise. As we went past the first floor, I glanced through an open doorway and saw rows of metal cots, each with a child in it. Most of them seemed to be crying. The nurse hurried us on, and we came to the landing of the second floor. Three rooms opened off it: two dormitories, crammed with cots, and another room which had a low table, infant chairs and a wooden climbing frame. The climbing frame had more chairs stacked in it, evidently for storage, and a few toys were tied to the bars. Round the walls of each of the rooms were fastened a variety of toys: activity centres, dolls, teddies, cars, even books. They were all well above child height, and appeared to be in very good condition. The room with the table and chairs was empty, and all the noise was coming from the dormitory straight ahead of us. Without waiting for permission I walked through the door, and immediately the noise increased.

There were about twenty-four cots in the room, nearly all occupied by ragged, emaciated little boys and girls. Their shaved hair made their heads look far too big for their undernourished bodies. Some of the children were standing up, holding on to the bars and screaming. Others were rocking backwards and forwards, banging their heads against the end of the cots. Still more were just lying or sitting silently, their large dark eyes blank in their strained grey faces. They twisted their hands in front of them, or hung them through the bars of the cots as if imploring someone to take notice of them. Many of the children had deformed limbs or faces. One at least was blind. Although they were all together in the room, there was a dreadful sense of loneliness and desolation. The sheets in the cots were soiled with urine or faeces, and the smell was overpowering. I felt nausea rising in me, not just at the disgusting conditions but at the tragedy of such suffering young lives. Behind me, Libs' eyes had filled with tears and Mihaela, her face completely white, had turned away. A nurse came out of an inner room and asked a question. Nicu, who had been talking to the other nurse, came in to explain our presence. He too looked shocked and upset. I remembered Rodica telling me that he had young children of his own.

The nurse pointed to one of the furthest cots, and I saw a child sitting there, tapping his head. It was Robert. With a cry, I hurried along to him, followed by the others. I had been worried that I wouldn't recognise him after such a long time. I reached into the cot and picked him up tenderly. He was wearing a curious combination of pyjama top and ribbed tights, and he was very wet and dirty. He was even lighter and frailer than I remembered. Some of the bigger children started to climb out of their cots to come to us, but the two nurses shouted at them and roughly put them back in again.

Robert sat very stiffly on my knee, unable to understand what was happening to him. Elizabeth talked to him, holding his hand, while I cuddled him. Mihaela was in tears, unable to cope with the shock of what she was seeing. I realised that while we were prepared in some ways for the orphanage by what we'd seen on television, she had no idea at all what went on behind the walls of the Casa de Copii – Romania had never broadcast its shame to its people. But no television images, however vivid, could match the horror of the reality.

Robert tapped his head, looking at us vacantly. He seemed much worse than when Graham had visited him in September. From my bag, I produced a small toy I had brought with me. That got a response! His hand shot out and he grabbed the little plastic car and held it tightly. His brown eyes showed a flicker of interest as he looked at it. But then he started to tap his head again. The lawyer spoke to Mihaela who in turn told Elizabeth and me that we had to go. It was the children's rest time. Libs turned the sheets round, trying to find a clean dry patch, and I lifted Robert back into the cot. He lay on his side, still clutching the car, his eyes following us as we waved goodbye and left the room.

We stood on the landing, listening to the nurses shouting at the children, not knowing what to do next. Nicu started back down the stairs, and we followed, silent with the emotional shock of what we had just experienced. We did not speak to Dr Popescu again, but left the building straight away, glad of the icy air to clean our mouths and lungs of the stench. As we walked back towards the Judecatorie, Nicu spoke to Mihaela, and she tried to explain to us. Dr Popescu would not allow the required medical without documentation from the Committee, and they were not authorising anything until the new adoption law was brought into force in the New Year. Meanwhile, we could not proceed with the adoption without the medical and social reports. We had reached an impasse.

'But we *do* have a piece of paper from the Committee. Surely that is enough authority for her to do the medical? If we wait for them to start up again, it could be months . . .' Mihaela consulted the lawyer.

'The paper is OK. That is why you can see Robert. But not enough for medical.' It was so frustrating.

'Is there nothing more we can do? We must get him out of there.'

She shrugged. 'He try.' I couldn't decide whether that statement was meant to refer to the past or the future.

Over the next few days, our lives took on something of a pattern. We were very concerned not to intrude on Mihaela and Adrian, so we went out for a good part of each day, visiting the orphanage and then going for long walks round the town. The first action every morning was to discover when hot water would appear. In this part of the country, hot water was available for only two hours a day. It was controlled centrally, and no one had any choice in the matter. There was a schedule, detailing when the hot water would be available, but this was not always reliable. So every morning, at various times, the cry of *apa calda!* would go up, and everyone would rush to fill the bath, the sink and the washing-up bowl. At the end of the two hours, the hot-water tap would dry up and remain lifeless until the next session. Sometimes we missed it altogether because we were not up early enough. I realised how much I took hot water for granted back in England. Even if people didn't have it on supply all the time, at least they could choose when to have it. And think of the difficulties of keeping young children clean with only two hours' worth of hot water a day. Eventually, after either a hot or cold wash and a breakfast of bread and cheese, we would put on our layers of clothes and set off.

We kept calling at the lawyer's office, but each time we tracked him down he had little to report. Stalemate prevailed, with everyone requiring a document that someone else refused to produce. Nicu had rung the Adoption Committee, without giving too much away – there was a danger that they might say that the case was not valid at all – but they had not been very helpful. Their view was that we must go with whatever the court decreed. The court was rigorous in its requirements for the adoption hearing to take place, and we could not get all the documents because the Orphanage Director wanted new authorisation from the Committee which the Committee was not yet prepared to issue. Everyone seemed immovable, despite the lawyer's arguments and our pleadings. But at least we were free to come and go at the orphanage, and already time spent with Robert was beginning to bear fruit.

It was still a nauseating and emotionally draining experience to go in there. I had to force myself, every time, to walk through the doors. The children mobbed us when we went into Robert's *salon*, as the dormitories were called. They clawed at us, climbing up our legs and clinging to our arms, rubbing their shaved heads and filthy faces on our clothes. But Robert remained in his cot, not showing any reaction when we arrived. He still looked vacantly into the distance and tapped his head. I could see that Elizabeth was increasingly concerned about him as the week wore on. Her medical training made her aware of signs that would mean nothing to me, but she refused to discuss it, maintaining that it was impossible to tell what, if anything, was wrong with him without a battery of properly conducted tests. I knew that we could never get those in Romania.

Robert was clearly scared of the other children and made no attempt to communicate with them. He could hardly walk, and tottered around like an eighteen-month-old. Yet there were signs of hope as well. He began to respond to us when we played with him, watching us all the time, and obviously enjoyed sitting on our laps. One morning, as I tried to play cars with one of the other children, I watched Libs put out the building blocks she had been playing with the day before. Robert looked at them for a while and then, slowly and carefully, he began to put one block on top of another to build a tower.

'Look, he's doing it!' I called in excitement. 'He's remem-

bered what you showed him, and he can do it!' He was only
doing what every normal toddler does, yet it seemed a remarkable step forward.

At that moment, a crowd of other children rushed in and
knocked the tower down, snatching the blocks and running off.
Robert clutched the block that was still in his hand and tapped
his head. He did not react in any other way to this vandalism of
his work. I thought of the shrieks of indignation we'd have had
at home, and realised afresh how different Robert was.

We never felt able to stay very long in the orphanage.
Usually after a while one of the carers would take Robert off
on some excuse or other and we would be left to make our way
out again. On a few occasions we took a diversion into some of
the other salons, and sometimes managed to take photographs
of what we saw. There were extremely ill children in one room.
They were just lying in their cots listlessly, unattended and
unloved. One, Elizabeth suspected, was near death. He lay with
his eyes closed, no cover on him, completely alone. We stroked
his face and murmured words of love, praying comfort for him.
Then, choked with emotion, we left before we were discovered
and banned altogether from the orphanage.

We wandered back towards the town centre, drawn to the
bakery and lunch. Mealtimes were flexible at Mihaela and
Adrian's, and the cold made us constantly hungry. We had
brought lots of foodstuffs with us, and bought bread for us all
most days, but we did not want Mihaela to feel under pressure
to be producing meals for us all the time. So we usually bought
a snack at lunchtime and ate it in the open air before exploring
the area a bit more.

We noticed very many people walking around with Christmas trees tucked under their arms. They seemed to be as much
an accessory as a shopping bag. Nowhere, though, was there a
decorated tree. Some had been left on balconies or in the halls
of apartment blocks, and some were leaning against walls in
shops, but they were all untrimmed. Yet there were only two

weeks to go to 25th December. I contrasted this with England, where decorations could be seen months before.

'I know,' said Libs, 'let's get a tree for Adrian and Mihaela.'

'Good idea, but we'd better check that they haven't already got one somewhere else.' We had discovered that Romanians generally have a network of contacts from whom they obtain the necessities of life. Adrian and Mihaela both had relatives in the outlying villages who had smallholdings, providing meat and dairy produce for those who could come and get it. Maybe they had a relative who grew trees! On every street corner there were piles of Christmas trees, attended by a fur-hatted salesman. The prices were ridiculously low by Western standards. I could see that Libs was longing to walk round town with a tree tucked under her arm. After consultation with Mihaela we chose a healthy-looking specimen and proudly carried it back to the apartment.

A less charming aspect of Christmas in Romania soon became apparent. I had noticed that many of the horses and carts in the town were carrying pigs, which looked quite quaint, an illustration of the mixture of modern and traditional which prevails there. I had also been aware in the past few days of a curious smell in the air, a sort of burning. It was not until we were walking down a street one day, exploring the upper part of Alba, that we discovered what was happening. We heard frantic squeals coming from behind a gate, squeals which ended very suddenly. We peered through and saw a group of people, some of them carrying knives, bending over the carcass of a pig. As a vegetarian I found this particularly distasteful, but realised that my opinions were in a definite minority here. Continuing our walk, we came across another group, this time on the pavement, clustered round a dead pig and wielding what looked like a blowtorch. They were burning the bristles off the body. The smell that I had been vaguely aware of all week was extremely strong. Suppressing a shudder of distaste, I picked my way over the rivulets of blood and carried on. Elizabeth, the nurse, craned her neck to get a better look. She seemed to find my reactions highly amusing.

When we got back to the flat, Mihaela was busy in the kitchen. Her dictionary was open on the chair beside her.

'Special food today,' she smiled.

'Ooh, lovely,' we responded. 'What is it?'

'Sausages!' she replied. Libs choked her laughter down, unable to look at my face. I summoned up what I hoped was an enthusiastic smile. I had not told her that I was vegetarian; it seemed an offence to her loving hospitality, and I knew that obtaining food was difficult. I was just very grateful to her for looking after us. I prayed for grace to enjoy the food!

We felt as if we were getting to know Adrian and Mihaela quite well. In the dark evenings, when nothing more could be done in the town, we would sit around exchanging information as best we could about our different ways of life. Mihaela's English was improving noticeably, and my Romanian was beginning to come together a little. Mostly, though, we tried to explain things through mime and gestures, which often had hilarious results. Adrian was a gifted musician; several evenings, he got out his guitar and we had an impromptu concert of songs and hymns from our respective churches. He would play their favourites, and then Libs would play ours, with everyone joining in as best they could. It was great fun and, in a lovely way, very worshipful as well. Sometimes Neli, Adrian's cousin, came down from her flat upstairs, and once Rodica and Alexandru called. It was wonderful to enjoy the company of these new friends.

The only thing marring my enjoyment was the uncertainty surrounding Robert's adoption, and his unhappiness in the Casa de Copii. The week was passing all too quickly, and though it had been extremely valuable to be here we were no nearer to getting him out. It didn't look as if my secret hope of a miracle was going to occur. The last day of our stay arrived, and we had not been able to make sufficient progress to take him with us. It had been very important to spend the time with him, and to make it clear to all the authorities that we were still actively pursuing the case, but it still felt dreadful to leave him behind. I held him close for a last hug, and my eyes filled with tears. It was almost unbearable to walk away from him. I didn't know when the legalities would be resolved, but I promised that I would come back for him one day soon.

Back in England, the shops were full of gaudy decorations and canned music blaring out 'Jingle Bells' and 'I'm Dreaming of a White Christmas'. Supermarket shelves groaned with every kind of food you could imagine, and the cash desks at the toy shops were congested with overflowing trolleys pushed by fond parents determined to outdo each other in the present-giving stakes. The town swarmed with last-minute shoppers, spending more than they really wanted to ('After all, it *is* Christmas!'). And the baby born in a smelly stable in conditions of poverty hardly got a look in at all. Perhaps a few carols might be sung to remind the nation of the story, but mainly he was forgotten, submerged in sentiment and elbowed out by a consumerist Santa.

In Romania, people killed their pig for a special celebration and worried that there was not enough money for bread, let alone gifts for each other. Their appreciation was great for any small extra which might come their way. For hundreds of children, including Robert, Christmas Day would be the same as any other, confined to a cot, ignored by all, with perhaps a short time competing for space in the 'playroom'. No pretty Christmas tree for them, no piles of presents, no stockings hanging up. The tattiest toy would be precious in their eyes, and a smile or hug of love the best gift of all.

I could hardly cope with the contrast between the two cultures. I wanted to give our children a happy and exciting Christmas, but the memories of what I had so recently seen were too stark and raw for me to be comfortable or at peace. We had always made Christmas a special yet simple celebration, focusing on the Nativity story and the wonderful gift God gave to the world. Yet even within the comparative non-extravagance that we maintained, I recognised that we had so very much more than my friends in Romania. I walked round in a daze, my mind crowded with thoughts of the orphanage and the everyday poverty I had witnessed in that troubled country.

It was hard to respond to all the interested questions about my trip, because I couldn't describe adequately all that I had experienced. Everyone had been going about their normal business; however concerned they were, they couldn't conceive of the conditions there. I felt quite isolated, and only wanted to talk to people who had actually been to Romania, and who therefore understood. My friends were very patient with me, and were as supportive as possible.

Just before the end of term, it was the infants' nativity play at the boys' school. As I watched these little ones acting out the Christmas story, so innocent and happy, images of other children came into my mind; children rocking in their cots, dark eyes hopeless and resigned, children attacking each other, children crying themselves to sleep in misery. Tears filled my eyes and I started to weep silently, overwhelmed with grieving for lost innocence and childhood.

When the celebrations were over, we began to pursue the case once more. It proved to be an extremely difficult task. The bureaucratic habit of passing enquiries on to another department was practised diligently by both Britain and Romania, the only difference being that Romania didn't even pretend to be helpful. We came across sympathetic people, irritated people and just plain rude people, but no one seemed able to further our cause. Sometimes there appeared to be a breakthrough – perhaps someone who would speak for us to the Committee – but then we would hear that it had come to nothing. Our emotions were on a rollercoaster of hope and disappointment. We wrote to our MP, to Mrs Bottomley, the then Minister of Health, to the Foreign Office and to the British and Romanian Embassies. We also wrote to Peter Thurnam MP because we heard that he was taking up the cause of inter-country adoption. But though we received sympathetic replies from all of these, they merely said that there was very little they could do. The position was that, although a new law concerning adoption had been passed in Romania the previous summer, no adoptions were being allowed to proceed until separate treaties had been signed with all participating countries. I discovered this from a helpful gentleman at the Department of Health, Mike Brennan.

'So when is Britain signing this treaty?' I asked.

'Ah, well, that I can't say,' he replied. 'It's not up to us, you see. I am in discussions with the Romanian government and the Adoption Committee.' (I bet he didn't have to stay all day in the waiting-room!)

'What sort of things will be in the treaty?'

'Well, that's what we are discussing. The Romanians are researching ideas from different systems to cover inter-country adoptions. They are going into it quite rigorously.' I didn't like the sound of that. Although we wholeheartedly agreed that there must be regulations to protect the best interests of the child, I feared that the Romanians might have a hidden political agenda in all their treaty-making.

There was quite a network of people who had adopted Romanian children or who, like us, were stuck in the middle of the process. Some had been trying to adopt for even longer than we had. A few had been forced to give up. This network had become an informal support group, fulfilling a need for people to talk to others who understood the situation and who might have some useful advice or help. Rumours began to fly around the grapevine about what would be required once the treaty was signed. No one knew what the time scale was, and the Committee was now refusing to take calls from individuals.

We were told that we had to deal with our own 'agency'. There must have been hundreds if not thousands of us, from all over the world, waiting to adopt, all wanting information, so it was understandable that the Committee had opted out. Phoning Romania was always a problem, anyway. It often took nine or ten tries just to connect with the country, and then you didn't always get through to the right number. If you were fortunate enough to get this far, the background noise and slight speaking delay made it very difficult to have a coherent conversation. I decided that I was quite glad not to have to ring the Committee every week.

The days passed in the enjoyable busyness of family life. Joel had started at infants' school the previous term, and now Barnaby was beginning in the nursery unit at the same school. Like the others he settled in well, and waved goodbye happily every morning. It seemed strange to have just one child at home, if only for two hours, and I made the most of it, knowing that if – no, when! – we got Robert, it would be even more difficult to get individual time with each of the boys. For Nathanael, it would be like suddenly acquiring a twin, as there were only eight months between them.

People in our village of Poppleton were interested and concerned in our attempts to adopt and we very much appreciated their support. However, during these months, when there seemed to be nothing happening and nothing we could do to make it happen, I found the kindly enquiries very difficult to handle. It was impossible to express the horror of what I had seen to someone who had never been there, nor to convey the complexities of the bureaucratic and legal process that we were up against. I could see that most people could not understand why we had not adopted Robert already. I felt sure that most also thought that we had failed in our attempt, and that we would never now be able to adopt him. It was easy to slip into that way of thinking myself. But I truly believed that the Lord had told us to adopt a Romanian child and had led us to Robert, so I clung to that belief, and told those who asked that we were trusting God to make the adoption possible, even though the governments seemed to be putting up obstacles. It was the truth, but sometimes, after yet another negative phone call, I found it hard to believe. My faith that God was in control and that he *would* fulfil his purposes was being severely tested. But then, faith is, by definition, a holding on to belief in the dark, when you cannot see the way ahead: 'Now faith is being sure of what we hope for and certain of what we do not see' (Heb. 11:1). So we continued to state that we would be getting Robert soon, not out of stubbornness but out of an inner conviction that it really would happen.

Our families had varying reactions to the whole situation. My parents, Keith and Margaret, were concerned that we might be taking on too much, that four children were quite enough without adding another child with special needs. And my father was worried that we were bringing into the family someone of whom we knew nothing, who might bring us much grief in one way or another. But despite these concerns, which we respected, they were generous in their support, and my mother particularly maintained an active interest in what was happening. Graham's father and stepmother were more detached. We felt that they didn't really approve of what we were attempting to do, but their attitude seemed to be that it was our decision and they would let us get on with it. It was not always easy to press on when we sensed unspoken fears and disapproval from those we loved and whose opinions we valued, but we felt compelled to continue.

We made contact with a charity, Project Alba, which worked in Robert's orphanage, and I asked if it would be possible to find out how Robert was getting on. Libs and I had met some of the aid workers briefly while we were there in December, and they had given us the address of their headquarters. They worked mornings in the orphanage and afternoons in the local hospital. Most of the volunteers were qualified in some relevant area and hoped to pass on their expertise to the Romanian workers. The administrator of the charity, based in the Midlands, gave me the phone number of a girl called Penny who was out there at the time. After several attempts I succeeded in making contact, and she was happy to talk. She knew who Robert was, but was not very encouraging in her report. He had been ill during the winter, with a chest infection she thought, and had been given some antibiotics. He was still very pale and listless, and seemed to be getting more and more withdrawn. Apparently he spent most of his time isolated from the others. She said that she would keep an eye on him, and that I was welcome to phone again. As I put the phone down, my instinct was to catch the next plane and go to him. Common sense prevailed, of course, but my heart ached for that poor ill lonely little boy. I continued to phone the Project Alba team from time to time, but the picture remained much the same. The girls took an interest in him, but I could tell that they felt that Robert was regressing. This continuing bad news weighed heavily on us, and we prayed that God would engineer a breakthrough in all the bureaucracy, so that we could rescue him from his dreadful circumstances.

We also kept in touch with some friends we had made on our travels, Richard and Ruth Monk. We had first seen them in May, on the plane, but really only to smile at in passing. Then Libs and I had got to know them much better as we all waited for the plane home in December. True to form, the plane was delayed several hours, and many of the passengers had gravitated together to keep our spirits up. In the end, we took this literally: one of the passengers, a friendly Romanian with business in England, opened a bottle of whisky, and we all shared a tot to keep warm. There was no heating in the airport and the temperature was well below freezing. We felt sorry for the transit passengers from Thailand, who arrived looking tanned in shorts and brightly coloured shirts! Richard and Ruth told us a little about their own attempts to adopt. They had been allocated a child in March, a few months before us. She was an older child, Elena, aged five, from Bacau in the north of the country. Richard and Ruth had been unable to have children of their own, despite numerous tests and treatments, but wanted good to come out of this sadness by helping a child who was in great need. They too were having great trouble in obtaining all the documents required, and had not yet got the mother's signature of consent. In the months of blankness that followed, it was good to talk to them, and share any news and feelings that we had. Richard and Ruth were not Christians, but seemed to take some comfort from our belief that somehow God would sort things out.

We heard from Rodica and Alexandru that they had managed to get a medical visa to come to England for Andrei to be treated. There was still no real certainty as to what was actually wrong with him, but they felt sure that the more advanced technology and training in England would be able to diagnose the problem. The consultant had agreed to waive fees, and they were going to stay with their English friends who had arranged the whole thing. We were delighted and relieved for them, and arranged to go and see them at a later date. Rodica was still very upset by all that had happened, and understandably was finding it hard to cope. Alexandru was coming over for a few weeks, but then he would have to return to Romania, leaving his wife and son behind. It was a hard situation for them all, made worse by the continuing uncertainty as to the seriousness of Andrei's condition. They had been given such a dreadful prognosis by the Romanian doctors that they had almost lost hope. But now, with the opportunity of treatment in England, they felt a new optimism. We kept in touch with them, wanting to support them as much as possible. And as far as our own problems were concerned, nothing seemed to be happening at all.

Then came the awful phone call. I had just returned from school, and was setting out some playdough for Nathanael, when the phone rang. It was our contact in the Foreign Office.

'Just to let you know that the treaty with Romania concerning inter-country adoption has finally been signed,' she said.

'So does that mean that we can go ahead at last?' I asked, my heart racing with excitement.

She hesitated. 'I'm afraid that there is a problem in your case. The new rules state that only families with two or fewer children can adopt.'

My knees gave way and I sat on the floor, my hands shaking. 'B–but that can't be right. We've been accepted by the Committee. We've nearly completed . . . I mean, we . . .'

'I'm sorry, but they say that anything which happened before the law change and new treaty doesn't count, unless you'd got your papers into court before 17th July 1991. You'd have to apply again, and they wouldn't accept you.' How could she sound so calm and businesslike? But then, she didn't know what it was like out there, what the rules were condemning a little boy to. She hadn't just lost a child.

I said goodbye and burst into tears. Nathanael toddled in and offered me a playdough cake. I gave him a hug and cried some more, unable to believe that Robert wouldn't soon be playing here as well. Still very upset, I dialled Graham's number, but he was in a meeting. Perhaps just as well, I thought in retrospect. It's not very helpful while you're at work to have a distraught female on the other end of the phone. Gradually, as I calmed down, my thoughts turned to the Lord, and I asked for *his* help. Suddenly, I felt amazingly peaceful, and the thought came to me that nothing that God had said had changed. The Romanians had altered their policy, but God hadn't said anything different. Did I believe that he had told us to adopt Robert? Yes, I did, and I still believed that. But maybe God was speaking through these circumstances, showing us that we had been mistaken. Yet it didn't feel that way, because it seems that when God makes his will clear, it is accompanied by an inner feeling of peace, whatever one's outer emotions are like. I did not have this inner peace about a decision to stop our adoption of Robert, and I did not believe such a decision came from God. If it did, then I wanted confirmation! I realised that we did not need to work out how God would fulfil his promise; we just needed to trust that he would.

By the time I managed to get through to Graham, I was feeling much calmer, though my stomach felt as if it had a lead weight in it, and I was able to prepare him for the shock of the news. Graham is a much more even-natured person than me, so he did not react with tears or shouting, but I could tell that he was extremely upset. There was a characteristic silence as he digested the implications, and then his voice trembled as we talked through our reactions. Like me, he couldn't bear to think of Robert wasting away in that orphanage. We held out little hope that anyone else would adopt him. The Romanians were obviously cutting down on the number of people they would allow to adopt, and Robert, as an older handicapped child, would not stand much chance. We both felt that we must keep fighting for him, but exactly how was too daunting a question at that moment. It had been hard enough to have faith that God would achieve his word when there was no news. It was even harder now that we had been told that the adoption was impossible. Yet, despite the circumstances and my emotional reaction to them, deep down was a certainty that Robert would join our family.

One kind friend, Val, had given us a lovely teddy for him. Rather than take it to Romania, where it would probably have disappeared, I had put it on the bureau as a reminder of our absent child. Whenever I caught sight of it I promised it that, one day, Robert would come and take it to bed with him. Sentimental perhaps, but such actions helped me to keep my faith strong at a time when it was very vulnerable. We were also helped tremendously by friends at church, who encouraged us to hold on to what we believed God had said to us, and who prayed regularly for us and for Robert. It was marvellous to be so supported by the larger family of the church.

When we were worshipping together one Sunday morning, God spoke to me clearly through the words of the song we were singing. The song was 'Oh Faithful God', and three lines in particular leapt out at me:

> You lift me up, and you uphold my cause.
> You give me life, you dry my eyes.
> You're always there, you're a faithful God.

It was as if God was confirming all that he had said to us. Yes, he would uphold our cause. I experienced a new confidence in the Lord, and felt strongly that I should speak out publicly what I believed. Then my mind kicked in. 'Wait until something has actually happened,' went my thoughts. 'It makes a more complete story that way. And if nothing happens, you won't have made a fool of yourself.' This was good logic, yet I knew that I had to speak now, before there was anything concrete to prove me right, about God's faithfulness to his word.

Before logic got the better of me I made my way to the front of the church, and when there was an appropriate break I told, very simply, of the current circumstances concerning Robert, and how difficult it was to match these recent developments with the calling we believed came from God, to adopt him. Basically, we were receiving two contradicting messages: God's, which was to rescue Robert, and the Romanian authorities', which was that we couldn't. It wasn't easy, when things looked so black, to declare publicly that we still believed that God wanted us to adopt Robert and that therefore we would. Yet as I did it I felt a tremendous confirmation that what I was saying would come true. I felt lighter in my spirit than I had done for a very long time. By fulfilling the spiritual principle of declaring God's word in faith, before it had come to pass, I had enabled power to be released, in the situation and in myself. Afterwards, several people told me that they also were in circumstances which seemed to be against what God wanted for them, and that what I had said had encouraged them to hang on to God and not give up believing that he would resolve things for them. It was exciting to hear this, and I realised yet again that the ripple effect of Robert's rescue would reach far more widely than we had ever imagined.

6

Back to square one?

Frustrated, I listened as the phone made its familiar crackling buzzing noises and then went dead. This was my third attempt to make contact with Romania that morning and I had failed each time. NASA had more success speaking to people in space! I slammed the receiver down and sat in disconsolate silence, pondering the deadlock we were in.

Over the weeks since we had heard the news about the treaty, we had kept up a barrage of phone calls to anyone whom we thought might be able to plead our case. Our argument was that we had been allocated a child when the Committee was still operating in May 1991, and that therefore we had a moral, if not legal, case to continue the adoption. The Committee was still not answering calls from individuals, so we tried the Foreign Office and the Department of Health. We also enlisted the help of the Pughs, to see if they could find out anything from their end, but they were as ignorant as we were, and feared that if they made too much fuss on our behalf they might have to give Ionela back to her orphanage, as they were only fostering her and had no legal rights. Our other friends, Ruth and Richard, were despairing about Elena, and had been considering the idea of Ruth taking some time off work to go to Romania again to try and sort things out. We decided that there was no point in us going out again until we had heard something definite. I tried Mike Brennan again, hating to pester but knowing that we had to keep a high profile.

He was as polite as ever, giving no sign of irritation at my perpetual phone calls.

'I am in fact going to Romania this week,' he told me, 'and I will bear your case in mind when I am with Dr Zugravescu.'

She was the President of the Adoption Committee. I thanked him with a heavy heart and no great hopes; we had been disappointed so many times before. I was therefore quite surprised when, the following week, Mr Brennan phoned me.

'Ah, Mrs Smith, I may have some good news.' My heart started to beat wildly.

'What news, exactly?'

'Well, I'm afraid that I'm not at liberty to say at present. However, as I shall be away on holiday for the next two weeks, the Committee have given you special permission to phone them on Wednesday morning at 9.00 a.m. British time.' I went numb with shock.

'But why? I mean, what are they going to say?'

'I'm sorry, Mrs Smith, I can't say any more, but if all goes well I think you will be pleasantly surprised.' On which enigmatic note, he wished me luck and rang off. I didn't even wish him a happy holiday! I was so excited that I couldn't settle down to anything. At last it looked as if the breakthrough we had been praying for was about to happen. I could barely contain myself! But as Graham, who generally has a more cautious and wise approach to life, reminded me, we should not assume anything yet. The Romanians had not maintained a good track record for keeping their word in this area, and we might be disappointed yet again. I agreed in theory, but kept wishing away the time until Wednesday arrived.

I arranged for one of my friends to take the children to school, so that I could start phoning before 9 o'clock. Never had the Romanian telephone system seemed more frustrating. After a quarter of an hour of noisy misconnections and number unobtainable sounds, I was ready to scream. Then I got through at last, and the line was *engaged*! My nervousness made me misdial the long number on several occasions, and I was beginning to wonder if I would ever get through. I imagined the Committee telling each other that we were obviously not interested after all, since we had not bothered to ring at the set time. Desperately I punched in the numbers again and this time, to my relief, the ringing tone started. It went on for what seemed an age.

'*Da?*' came a woman's voice. I pictured her in the office where I had been interrogated.

'*Vreau vorbi la Cristina Fulga, va rog,*' I managed, in dreadful Romanian. Cristina Fulga was the lady responsible for British adoptions.

'*Moment*' said the receptionist, and I waited, hardly breathing, until a different voice came on the line.

'Hello, this is Cristina Fulga.' I explained who I was, mentioning my conversation with Mike Brennan, and she immediately knew the case.

'Yes, the Committee has decided to support your adoption of Robert Toldea. You can come and collect our authorisation and complete the procedure.' She said it so calmly and without expression that I didn't take it in at first.

'W–when? I mean, *thank you*! But when will the document be ready?' I stammered, completely thrown by the news we had been longing to hear for so many months.

'It is ready now. You can collect it any time.' I thought rapidly. I didn't want them to have a chance to change their minds for any reason.

'Friday,' I said. 'I'll come the day after tomorrow.'

'Very well,' she agreed. 'We shall see you on Friday morning.'

I sat down, trembling, too shocked even to make a coffee. It had happened at last! God had done a miracle, and we had been given the go-ahead. This was what we had prayed for, and now that it had actually happened I couldn't believe it. After a while I pulled myself together, and thanked God for keeping his word. I was so excited that I was incoherent, both in my prayer and afterwards when I phoned Graham to tell him the good news. His joy and relief came clearly through the telephone. The waiting had been a strain for both of us. We began to make plans, our whole thinking changed by the turn of events. It was the last day of the spring term, and Graham's brother Barry and his family were coming to stay for the week before Easter. I hoped that they wouldn't take offence at my almost immediate disappearance!

I managed to get a flight booked for the next day, and started to pack, while at the same time trying to tidy the house, make up the beds and prepare meals ready for Barry and Hilary's arrival that evening. There were so many things to think of. I phoned the Pughs, to beg a bed for the following night, and they were as welcoming as ever. They were also incredulous at the Committee's change of heart. It gave them hope for their own adoption, though there was not quite the same pressure of time for them. They still had another year of John's contract to run, and Ionela was actually living with them. I also phoned Mihaela, who was a little startled at the short notice, but who said that of course I could come and stay for as long as I needed. I assured her that it would not be a very long stay. I collected food for her and the Pughs; there was still so much that was unobtainable in Romania. My bag was getting heavy. Then I suddenly realised that I would have to take lots of things for Robert, and so raced round buying nappies and baby food, and sorting out clothes and a few toys for him. I also borrowed a lightweight pushchair – one that folded up very compactly – as ours was a little too heavy, and anyway Nathanael would need it.

Telling the children that I was going away was easier than I anticipated. They were very excited to think that I was going to get Robert, and, because children tend to live in the present, they could not envisage what it meant for me to be away for a week, or perhaps two. They were also looking forward to the arrival of their three cousins, Naomi, Hannah and Rachael, and that took the edge off any feelings of sorrow at my departure. I was glad of the distraction for them. The next morning – early again! – I waved goodbye to everyone and stowed the overweight bag and the pushchair into the car. A good friend, Martin, was giving me a lift to Stansted on his way down south on business. Even the smallest details had fallen into place. I was glad to share some of the journey with this cheerful young man who, with his wife Clare, had always encouraged us in our adoption plans.

It was 16th April 1992, nearly a year since we had embarked on this adventure, and now, at last, it was nearing a successful conclusion. I was nervous at what lay ahead, but excited and confident as well. The obstacles had finally been overcome.

Bucharest Airport was as much of a maelstrom as ever. I found my luggage and stood, a little bemused, wondering how to find my contact. Then I heard my name being called.

'You are Susan Smeet?' The questioner was a pretty dark-haired young woman wearing an East Coast Travel badge. She must have spotted my luggage labels. Thankfully I put down my bag. I still had not worked out the system for getting a trolley at the airport; they were all jealously guarded by porters and not available for individuals to use.

'Yes. Hello. I believe I am getting a lift with you?' She nodded. 'I just have to meet another passenger, and then we will go.' She hurried off, calling '*imediat*' over her shoulder as she went. I settled down for a long wait. Experience had shown that the literal and actual meanings of *imediat* were directly opposed to each other! Sure enough, it was over half an hour before Mara, the representative, returned, minus her other client. But it was so nice to be given a complementary lift into Bucharest that I didn't mind. I was glad that I had been introduced to East Coast Travel by Richard and Ruth. The company arranged special offers for aid workers (somehow, we qualified) and they had also booked my onward train ticket to Alba Iulia.

My excitement mounted as we rattled our way down now familiar roads. I thought how much easier things were this time compared to a year previously. Then we were complete strangers, with no idea of language or culture or the complexities we were up against. Now I had friends to go to, a small knowledge of the language and more confidence to find my way around. I realised how much I loved coming back to Romania. The country, for all the horrors I had seen and all the frustrations I had experienced, had captured my heart.

The Pughs had moved to a new apartment on the other side of Bucharest. It was near some of the embassies, in a pleasant leafy area of the city. As the car drew up beside an older-style apartment block, there were shouts from the third-floor balcony. All three girls were hanging over the edge, waving and calling. I waved back, suddenly overjoyed to see them. Though we had not known each other long, our friendship had become very close. Mair and the girls appeared at the door of the apartment block and we all hugged each other warmly. Mara drove off, after telling me to get in touch if I needed any further help with travel arrangements. We went upstairs in the lift, and I exclaimed in appreciation at their new apartment.

It was much bigger than the old one, and had an air of gracious elegance about it, despite Ionela's toys strewn about the place. The furniture was solid wood, carved ornately in the Middle-European style, and throughout the flat there were richly coloured rugs covering the floor. The small passage from the front door opened into a large entrance area with several rooms leading off it. There was a table, bed and wardrobe tucked away in one corner. Mair explained that they had thought it important for the older girls to have their own space, and Hannah had opted to sleep in this room. Rebecca's room was light and airy, but would have been too small to share on a long-term basis; it was to be my room while I was staying. Ionela shared with Mair and John, still in her cot. I made a mental note to remind Graham to get our old cot out, ready for Robert. A cot was the only home he had ever known. He would need that security when he first came out of the orphanage.

We settled down to a cup of tea, as English (and Welsh) people do, and caught up with each other's news. Mair and John had been in touch with the British Embassy for me, and had discovered that it was not open on Fridays. My plan to go there after I had been to the Committee would have to be changed. I couldn't possibly wait in Bucharest until Monday; I was bursting with impatience to see Robert and to set the wheels in motion for an adoption hearing. Mair was also concerned that the contact at the Embassy had been quite negative. It did not sound as if getting a visa and entry clearance would be straightforward. I brushed aside her concerns, feeling optimistic that, once I had the Committee's authorisation, there should be no problem in getting all the other required documentation. And I would surely be assured of support from the British side. Mair had dealt with the Embassy several times over various issues, and wasn't as confident, but we both agreed that entry clearance was not a priority at present.

Ionela came dashing into the dining-room, interrupting our deliberations with her insistence on showing me her toys. She had blossomed since I had last seen her, both physically and mentally. She was able to speak now, where once John and Mair had feared she might never talk. She was still using only one or two words at a time, but she was able to make herself understood and was obviously making progress. I played with her for a little while before the evening meal, and wondered whether Robert would ever get to this stage.

The next morning, Rebecca and I set off in her school taxi. The family had felt that the Romanian education system was too different for the girls – they would have to slot back into the British system in two years' time – and didn't want them to lose too much ground. They were unable to afford the fees for the International School in Bucharest and so, as a compromise, had entered the older children in a French school. Neither girl spoke French, which made lessons and friendships extremely difficult. Hannah, who had found it hard to settle in Romania anyway, could not adjust to school at all, and Mair and John decided to educate her at home, using material from Britain. Rebecca, on the other hand, quite enjoyed school and soon discovered that she was able to pick up French and understand the lessons. She was also becoming fluent in Romanian.

The taxi dropped her at the school, and continued to the Piata Vittoria with me. A sense of *déjà vu* overcame me as I walked towards the sentry box. This time I could claim an appointment, though it didn't do me much good. I was told to wait while Cristina Fulga was summoned to approve me, and then I had to surrender my passport before being allowed to follow her through to the Committee offices. I felt quite insecure without it. What if they wouldn't give it back? I would be an illegal alien, unable to prove my British citizenship, unable to claim protection from my country. My imagination was brought to a halt as we arrived at the offices.

Everywhere was empty, even the waiting-room. I remembered the hours we had spent there, the noise, the smoke and the atmosphere of tension. It was all gone, and the place seemed like any other set of slightly dingy offices. How odd it must feel, I thought, for the staff to be able to go in and out of the rooms without having to push through crowds of people, all shouting questions. We went into an empty office, and Cristina asked to see the home study, now a prerequisite for the Committee authorising any adoption. Our interview was constantly interrupted by telephone calls and I began to wonder if I would ever get the all-important piece of paper. She looked at the other documents, copies of those lodged in the court in Alba Iulia, and commented on the lack of medical and social reports. I explained that we had been trying for a long time to get a medical done and she nodded, picked up the phone, dialled a number from one on a long list and asked for Dr Popescu. The conversation seemed to be satisfactory, for she smiled as she put the phone down and told me that Dr Popescu would do the medical on Tuesday. It had taken her a few minutes to achieve what we had failed to achieve in a year.

Cristina seemed friendly towards me and genuinely pleased that we were now able to adopt Robert. I spoke a little about how he was when I last saw him, and was amazed to see tears in her eyes. Moved by her evident care, I took the precious authorisation, shook hands with her and promised to send some photographs of him when we got back to England. I was walking on air as I left the Committee offices, and even the sentry's surly glance could not dampen my spirits. I gave him a beaming grin as he returned my passport, and was rewarded with a small smile in response.

I was booked on the overnight train to Alba Iulia, and so had the afternoon and evening with the Pughs. Mair was busy with visitors when I returned. More than ever, their home was a focal point for the expatriate community, as well as for a growing number of Romanians. Having spent time with them, I could understand why. There was always a warm and welcoming atmosphere. It was a kind of oasis in what could unquestionably be a hostile environment at times. I baby-sat in the evening, so that John and Mair could go to a concert, and on their return John took me to the station. I was glad to have a *cuseta*, a sleeping berth, but the presence of five other people in the compartment, most of whom snored, was not very conducive to sleep. I dozed fitfully, aware again of how busy even the smallest stations seemed to be in the middle of the night. I had just (or so it seemed) drifted into a deeper sleep when the guard banged on the door and shouted, 'Alba Iulia!'

It was 5.45 a.m., far too early to arrive at Mihaela and Adrian's. I took a taxi to the *Cetate*, the old fortress centre of the town, where I knew there was a hotel with a cafe. It didn't open until 7.00 a.m., however, so I sat on a wet bench in the public gardens and waited in the drizzling rain for the day to begin. Two hours and a very strong cup of coffee later, I arrived, cold and wet, at Mihaela and Adrian's home. They were delighted to see me, and we greeted each other with great affection. As if in my honour, the *apa calda* had just begun, and I celebrated my arrival with a welcome hot bath. Mihaela had been studying English diligently since my last visit, and her grasp of the language had much improved, though the same couldn't be said of my Romanian. She told me that she was helped by television, which was now broadcasting many more English language programmes, with Romanian subtitles. (Imagine seeing *Dynasty* in Romania – a bizarre contrast of cultures!)

After breakfast and a chat, Mihaela and I went to the orphanage to visit Robert. With the authority from the Committee in my bag, I felt confident that there would be no problem, and indeed the staff remembered us and didn't ask to see the document. As it was the weekend, the director and senior nurses were not on duty. We went up the stairs and again were struck by the nauseating smell. In Salon 2, Robert's dormitory, there was chaos. Children were racing round, screaming. Others were fighting each other, and many were rocking backwards and forwards, hitting their heads on the walls or the cot bars. Two women in dressing-gowns were standing in a corner, occasionally shouting at one or other of the children. I couldn't see Robert.

As soon as they noticed us, the children crowded round, competing for our attention. They clamoured to be picked up, tugging at our clothes. Some of them tried to open our bags and feel in our pockets. I realised that my first reaction was one of alarm and even revulsion, and felt ashamed of myself. But these little two- and three-year-olds, *en masse*, were a daunting prospect. Without any of the normal parameters of childhood – love, touch, stimulation, freedom, discipline – they were like wild animals, unable to articulate the humanity within them. As I recovered from my initial shocked response, I was overwhelmed once more by the tragedy of their situation, and prayed for God's love and wisdom in dealing with them. At least they were out of their cots.

But where was Robert?

One of the *asistente* had come across to greet us and was busy scolding the children and pulling them away from us. Mihaela, who was very upset, explained who we were and asked to see Robert. The carer's manner relaxed and she moved towards the other room, beckoning us to follow.

'Sanducan!' she called, using Robert's second name. 'Sanducan! *Hai la Mama!*'

'She's calling me his mother,' I thought, and, ridiculously, felt like crying. Robert was sitting all alone in his cot. He was extremely pale, and his huge brown eyes looked solemnly at us with no flicker of recognition. He made an effort to get up, but then sat back down again, tapping his head. I picked him up and held him close.

'It's Mummy, come to take you home,' I whispered. His thin hands grasped my jumper and held on tightly. His clothes were soaked in urine and loose faeces, and he smelt terrible.

'Perhaps we can wash him,' I whispered to Mihaela, and she nodded and went off to ask the carer. When she came back, I carried him to a long trough-like sink and stood him in it. He began to whimper, looking frightened. When I stripped off the filthy woollen tights and top, he became very distressed. Murmuring soothing words, and helped by Mihaela, I turned on the tap. The water was cold. Robert screamed. Hurriedly, I washed off the worst and got him out. The *asistenta* had produced a threadbare towel and I gently started to rub him dry, shaken by his reaction to the wash. His little legs were like sticks, and he still had an unhealthy pot belly. Mihaela found some more clothes in a cardboard box in the corner, and we dressed him. He clung to me, and did not want to be put down.

Just then, the rest of the group were herded into the dormitory and started crowding round us again. There were angry shouts from the *asistente*, who pointed to the adjoining room, where the toilets were situated.

'I think we must go now,' said Mihaela. 'They are busy.'

Reluctantly, I moved back to Robert's cot. We had not spent that much time there, and I didn't want to leave him. He seemed so defenceless and lonely.

'I'll come back tomorrow,' I promised as I gave him a hug. 'We'll play with some toys.' He clung on as I leaned over to put him in his cot, and I had to prise his fingers off in order to leave him there. We waved and called goodbye as we left the room, but he didn't respond. His eyes were fixed on the bars of his cot.

Mihaela and I were glad to be out of the oppressive atmosphere of the orphanage. How did the children endure their lives there? So much unnecessary misery and suffering. I couldn't wait to release one at least of them. Perhaps it would all be settled by the end of the week.

My thoughts were interrupted by Mihaela's suggestion that we call in at the Simus' home, since it was so close. I agreed. Rodica was still in England with Andrei, but I was looking forward to seeing Alexandru again. When we got there, however, everyone except Domna Simu was out. It was lovely to see her, and we stayed for a while before setting off again. We had got about a quarter of the way home when the familiar minibus drew up beside us and there was Alexandru, smiling and offering us a lift. I was glad to have re-established contact with him so soon. For various valid reasons, our focus had shifted towards Mihaela and Adrian, but we would always value Alexandru and Rodica's friendship, and would never forget the vital part they had played in helping us to find Robert. We chatted on the way home, and he told us that Rodica was expected back some time next week. He looked very happy at the prospect. It was obvious that he had been under tremendous strain, and had missed his wife and baby son a great deal.

The next day was Sunday, Easter Sunday in England but not in Romania, where it would be celebrated the following week. I went with Mihaela and Adrian to their church. We arrived at the building at 10.00 a.m., to find that a prayer meeting had already been in progress for an hour. We had come in time for the Sunday School teaching slot, which was followed by preaching, some singing and then a baptism at the end for about *fifty* adults. I wished that the church at home was growing as fast. I noticed, though, that everyone seemed extremely serious. There were no expressions of joy or happiness in the whole three hours I was there, even when the new members were baptised. When I asked Adrian about this over lunch, he replied that they did feel joy, but that it was very deep within them. As we talked, I learnt that these Romanian Christians had a very strict attitude to life, one that bordered on the legalistic. They were shocked when I told them that we danced sometimes in our meetings, and that we raised our hands to the Lord. Then I reflected that there were English Christians too who would be equally shocked by such admissions. Mihaela and Adrian considered it a sin for a woman to wear make-up or jewellery, or for anyone to drink alcohol. It was good to share our different ways and opinions, secure in our mutual love for the Lord, and our respect for each other's understanding.

After lunch, Adrian decided that he would like to come with me to the orphanage. He had never visited one before, and Mihaela's reports had aroused his curiosity as well as his compassion. We walked down together, discovering to our surprise and pleasure that the children were in the *gradina*, a small grassy area at the back of the building. This area contained some rusty play equipment as well as trees and a few wild flowers. Some neighbouring houses had their small-holdings backing on to the gradina, and a group of children were standing by the fence, gazing in amazement at the pigs and hens they could see. We went through the gates and explained ourselves to the carers in charge, who were happy for us to stay. They made no attempt to play with the children, nor to arbitrate in the many fights and squabbles which broke out. Instead, they stood talking to each other, for the most part ignoring their charges. If a situation became too volatile, they

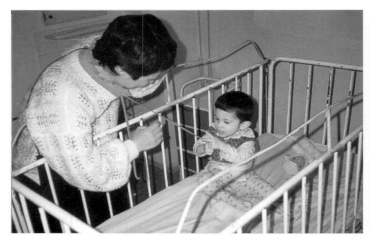

Our first meeting with Robert, Cimpeni, May 1991
(this and previous page)

Mihaela, Adrian, Rodica and Alexandru

The Simu Family

Robert, September 1991

Emilia (fourth from right) with the villagers
and lawyers, Horea

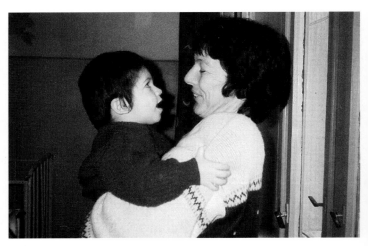

Robert and Sue at the orphanage in
Alba Iulia, December 1991

Robert and friends in the orphanage garden

Leagunul Nr 1, Alba Iulia

The reunion at Heathrow Airport, May 1992

Nathaniel welcomes Robert

Alba Iulia

would pull all the children away from each other, screaming vociferously, and sit them on the ground. Adrian was surrounded by clamouring children. It occurred to me that they were probably very unused to having a man in their midst. He looked shaken by all these demanding little hands and voices, and gestured to me helplessly. I smiled back, but didn't go to his aid because I was looking for Robert.

Although it was quite warm, the children were all wearing woolly hats, and it was difficult to distinguish one individual from another. Then I spotted him, sitting on his own by a bush. He was not trying to play with anything or anyone, but gazed seriously into the distance, like some great philosopher with a lot on his mind. I ran across and picked him up, hoping so much that he would recognise me. He reached out and grabbed my coat lapels. I would have to be content with that for now. Adrian, realising that this was Robert, came across to meet him, followed by a crowd of shouting toddlers. I imagined that the Pied Piper might have looked like this! We settled down to play with them, pushing them on swings, helping them on the slides, giving them piggy-backs and generally having fun. Adrian discovered that the play equipment had been installed by an American charity a year or so before. It was good to know that it was being used, although the children were no more encouraged to play in the gradina than they were in the so-called playroom. The disturbed behaviour patterns which had so upset me before were still very much in evidence.

After a while, the children were gathered up together to go back to their salon. It was bedtime. We followed them in, and so became part of one of the worst aspects of the orphanage routine. The children were sent into the toilet area in shifts and forced to sit on the rows of benches with holes in them, while the carers cleaned up any children who had already opened their bowels. The toilet area was vile. It stank of urine and faeces, and the walls and floors were filthy. In the middle, there were puddles of urine, in which the children splashed while they were supposed to be 'performing'. Most of these little ones were not toilet trained. They had no idea what they were meant to do there, so they made up their own activities, which included elbowing and kicking each other, pushing the next child off the bench, jumping up and down in the puddles and peering round the edge of the doorway until yelled at by the asistente. Once a group had finished in the toilets, each child was put into a cleanish pyjama top and tights and then dropped or tossed into a cot. Thin quilts were then distributed, one to each cot. These were quite smelly, and I thought about the potential cross-infection of bacteria from all this sharing of bedding.

The children did not wash their hands or clean their teeth, and there was no attempt to say goodnight to them individually. It was heartbreaking. I remembered bedtimes at home; special cosy times of story reading, talking, cuddles and prayers, times to make a child feel secure and loved. These children had no emotional input at all. Tears stung my eyes, and I busied myself with putting Robert into bed. He clung to me again, not wanting to be left, and I stroked his head, soothing him and praying over him. He lay very still, eyes fixed on the ceiling, while the other children shrieked and bounced and climbed out of their cots, and the asistente tried vainly to control them. Adrian and I left, unable to bear being there any longer, and walked home in virtual silence.

The next day, Mihaela and I went early to the Judecatorie to speak to Nicu. I needed to get the ball rolling as soon as possible if I was to get an adoption hearing by the end of the week. As usual, the place was crowded with a large cross-section of Alba society. We wove our way in and out of the noisy groups of people and waited outside Nicu's office door. A request to see him was sent in reasonably quickly, but it was nearly an hour before he emerged, looking more serious than ever. I could imagine that working in this kind of environment must be rather stressful. He smiled briefly but didn't look very pleased to see us. We shook hands, and after preliminary courtesies I explained that the Committee had given the go-ahead, and that we would like to have an adoption hearing as soon as possible.

The lawyer shook his head slowly and started a long explanation in Romanian. Mihaela listened and nodded, and then suddenly gasped and looked horrified. She came back with a question, and listened in growing disbelief to the answer. I endeavoured to glean a few words, desperate to find out what they were talking about.

'What is it?' I asked her urgently. 'What's going on?' Mihaela was pale, her jaw clenched with some emotion I could not quite define.

'It's the mother,' she said. 'Emilia. She has come to the court and taken away her . . . her . . .' she struggled to get the right word, '. . . permission.'

I looked blankly at her, unable to grasp her meaning at first.

'I don't understand . . . you mean that Emilia . . .'

'She say you cannot adopt Robert any more, so the court cannot allow it.' For a moment everything went black, and there was a roaring in my ears. Surely this must be a bad dream? I shook my head, and saw Mihaela and Nicu looking at me with concern.

'B–but *why*? Why has she changed her mind? And anyway, we have authority from the Committee to adopt him. Surely the court will recognise that?' Mihaela spoke to Nicu, who answered in the negative.

'It is the law that the mother must give her permission. Nothing can change that.'

'But she has never been a mother to him!' I burst out. 'Why should she have the power to decide his future when she hasn't seen him since he was three weeks old?'

Nicu shrugged. 'I am sorry,' he said.

'What can we do?' I asked, feeling at a total loss. 'I *can't* give up now.' All that we had worked for over the past year had been obliterated. We were back to square one, no further on than that first day when the doctor had commanded us to find the mother, and she had refused her consent. We had questioned, persuaded, cajoled the authorities and finally succeeded in gaining their permission, and now it was all for nothing. And in a building near by, a small child lay gazing at the ceiling, condemned by a mother he never knew to lose his only chance of freedom and love.

I could tell that the lawyer was sympathetic, though he found it hard to communicate this. He spoke for a while to Mihaela and then, with a farewell bow and kindly smile to me, he hurried off. Mihaela sighed deeply, more affected than I had realised by the devastating news.

'He will try to help,' she said. 'You must make him your lawyer by law, then he can work for you alone.'

'What can he do?' I asked eagerly, seizing on the slight hope offered.

She shrugged. 'Perhaps he can persuade the mother again. *Nu stiu.*' It was one of her favourite sayings, meaning 'I don't know'. Well, I didn't know the way out of this either, but God did, and somehow, I was convinced, he would show us a way to rescue Robert after all. We walked home for lunch, and afterwards I spent some time reading the Bible and praying. I found it hard not to cry. Adrian came and sat by me with his Bible and turned to Psalm 37, indicating that I should do the same. He told me that as he had been praying about the situation, he felt God was telling him to encourage me with these verses:

> Delight yourself in the Lord
>> and he will give you the desires of your heart.
> Commit your way to the Lord;
>> trust in him and he will do this:
> He will make your righteousness shine like the dawn,
>> the justice of your cause like the noonday sun.

Be still before the Lord, and wait patiently for him;
    do not fret when men succeed in their ways,
    when they carry out their wicked schemes.
Refrain from anger and turn from wrath:
    do not fret – it leads only to evil.

(Ps. 37:3–8)

It was exactly as if the words had been written with me in mind! Now I had to choose to believe them. God would uphold the justice of my cause, and I had to be at peace and know that he had the power to overrule the schemes of evil men. Adrian and I prayed together. Then, feeling much better, I set off on my own to see Robert.

The orphanage looked as forbidding as ever and I pushed through the doors quickly, bracing myself against the smell. When I got to the second floor, I met an English girl, Julie, working for Project Alba. Unlike the other volunteers, she was spending most of her time in the orphanage rather than dividing it equally with the hospital. It was marvellous to meet someone who was English. My Romanian was improving all the time, as I worked hard at learning it, but trying to communicate through a language barrier all the time was quite a strain. We were chatting together on the landing when we were approached by one of the carers, a lovely young girl called Maria, whom I had met a few times before. She appeared upset, and stood in front of the door to the playroom as if barring it. I looked enquiringly at her and asked, 'Robert?' She shook her head.

'The *directora* say no. No see Robert.'

'But why not? I have been before with no trouble.' I turned to Julie. 'Do you know why I can't see him?' She looked puzzled.

'I'm afraid not. I can't imagine why she should change her mind.' Maria spoke in Romanian, but I couldn't understand her and Julie didn't speak Romanian at all. The aid workers usually had an interpreter working with them. My mind began to race. Perhaps the director had heard from Emilia or the law courts that the consent had been withdrawn. Maybe she was going to transfer him. I peered through the glass of the door. There he was, standing alone near the table. Maria drew in her breath as he saw me and smiled spontaneously. He began to stagger towards me. I burst into tears. At last he had recognised me, and I was not allowed to see him.

Maria, in tears herself, opened the door a crack, and I knelt down and hugged him close, never wanting to let him go. 'Be still before the Lord and wait patiently for him. Do not fret when men succeed in their ways. The justice of your cause will shine like the noonday sun.' The words floated through my mind, calming my emotions and bringing an amazing inner peace. I blew my nose and let go of Robert. Maria led him back into the room, and I stood waving to him through the door. The pain was terrible.

7

Suffer the little children

'We must go and speak to the director!' said Mihaela, as I finished telling her the sorry tale. 'There must be some mistake.'

'I don't think so,' I said, too worn down by all the recent events to apply my normal optimism and faith. 'I've lost him legally, and now I can't even see him.' Mihaela looked at me in dismay. She was not used to seeing me so dispirited.

'Don't give up!' she said, giving me a hug. 'He is not lost yet!'

The next morning, after a very early start to catch the hot water, Mihaela and I went down to the orphanage to see the director. It felt somewhat akin to bearding a lion in its den. In fact, my worst fears were not realised, and we had a relatively good interview with her. Leah, the translator, was there, and once Dr Popescu had seen the document of authorisation from the Committee she changed her attitude completely. She gave permission for me to see Robert at any time, and agreed to do the medical soon. There was no mention of Emilia or the legal state of play. I couldn't understand why she had stopped me from seeing Robert, since Cristina Fulga had spoken to her on the phone about him. I could only assume that I had transgressed the rules by going to see him without seeking her consent first. I was tremendously relieved that the obstacle which had seemed so huge last night had been removed. We smiled and said thank you, elated by this small victory.

The legal battle would, I suspected, prove much harder. We hurried along for our appointment with Nicu, paying some money into the court beforehand. This secured the services of Nicu as my lawyer. He would not receive any of the money himself, but was paid a standard salary from the state. After the usual long wait to see him, we went eventually to the office of the President of the Court. There, we did something official which I assumed was the resubmission and acceptance of our papers into the court. It was frustrating not knowing exactly what I was doing. I had to trust the lawyer with so much. I was like a blind person being led on an unknown path. And everything I signed was legally binding. This was scary! But I realised that if I trusted God in this situation, then I could trust the person he had sent to help us. I shivered at such an uncharacteristically simplistic approach, but acknowledged that this was what was required at the moment.

We also visited the Municipal Prefect, the person responsible for producing a social report on Emilia. This was a legal requirement for the adoption, as was our home study. Domnul Cornel, a short thickset man, seemed sympathetic. He marvelled over the length of our home study, and asked to see a copy of the translation when it was ready. He agreed to do a social report on Emilia, which would necessitate a visit to Horea but, he said, it would take two weeks. I was horrified, knowing that things often took much longer than the time estimated. We tried to impress on him the urgency of the situation, but he did not seem to be persuaded. The Prefect was evidently a prestigious man; Nicu was quite deferential in his manner towards him.

I began to consider going home without Robert and returning in a few weeks, when everything was ready. Yet we had not even got Emilia's consent. I couldn't leave without that. Somehow, I would have to stick it out here until Robert was legally my child. I felt really homesick and longed to see Graham and the boys again. The emotional upheaval of the past few days was beginning to take its toll.

The rest of the week passed in a flurry of activity. We had to arrange the visit to Horea and find transport for it. Mihaela and Adrian did not own a car, and Alexandru was busy all week at work and was not able to take us. Adrian said he would try some friends in the church, or possibly his brother Simion. It was a great deal to ask anyone, and I suggested hiring a car or taxi, but they looked at me as if I was mad.

We also had to complete the medical. Dr Popescu kept to her word and wrote a medical report on Robert, but for some reason Nicu did not feel that it was sufficient for the purposes of the court. Accordingly, he took Robert and me up to the Polyclinic attached to the hospital for another examination. Robert was frightened in the car and terrified of the doctor. The examination was rough to the point of brutality, especially when his temperature was taken rectally, and he screamed throughout. I was distressed by his suffering and by my own impotence in the situation.

When I wasn't spending time with Robert in the orphanage, I was in the law courts or trekking round to the house of Daniela, the official translator, with more documents for her to work on. Not only did I need Romanian translations of the British documents, I was also required to send English translations of Romanian documents to the British Embassy for the entry visa. I spoke on the phone to Ms Hitchens, the lady responsible for granting entry clearance, and she appeared somewhat negative about it. She listed all sorts of requirements, and warned me that it would take a long time to process. She also said that I would need the entry visa before I could have an adoption hearing. I didn't understand that – it had not been mentioned by Nicu – but I didn't argue. I was more concerned to make her realise how urgent the case was. She, like Domnul Cornel earlier, was not to be moved.

My irritation was tempered by the reflection that she had probably had hundreds of people all pleading special treatment. When the first wave of prospective adopters had come into the country, the Embassy had been flooded by people desperate to obtain entry clearance and get home. A number of these had not gone through the due processes of law, and were infuriated when Embassy officials blocked or delayed their applications.

Many of the staff had been on the receiving end of tirades of frustration and abuse from people who had reached the end of their tether. I understood her caution, but I was also beginning to identify with those who lost their tempers with British bureaucracy. I would have to go down to Bucharest and visit the Embassy in person. For now, though, I was happy to forget about that element of the adoption because far more pressing was the prospect of meeting Emilia again.

Despite an early start, it was 11.30 a.m. before we set off from Alba Iulia along the beautiful road to Cimpeni. We had collected the borrowed car, met up with Nicu and waited while he did some last-minute work, searched and then waited for Domnul Cornel, and finally chased round the town looking for petrol. All the garages had enormous queues; in the end we had gone to Nicu's apartment and filled up with some that he had stashed in his garage. Needless to say, I was becoming more and more impatient with the delays. My nerves were on edge and I was tired from accumulated loss of sleep. Mihaela and I, squashed in the back of the small car with the portly municipal prefect, did not feel much like conversation. Moreover, the swaying of the car round the steep bends in the mountain road was beginning to make me feel quite sick. I opened the window a little, and noticed Domnul Cornel's worried look as I did so. After a while, he asked for it to be closed again.

I tried to concentrate on the beautiful countryside: the lush green pastures splashed with the colours of spring flowers, the thickly forested mountains bursting into life as the greenery unfurled. But my mind was on the ordeal ahead. Would Emilia be there? Would she maintain her refusal to consent to the adoption? What could I say to her to make her change her mind? The questions buzzed round like annoying insects, and I was glad when at last the uncomfortable journey was over and we stopped by a cluster of houses. Ahead of us, the muddy track wound up the hill. I remembered the trouble that

Alexandru's minibus had got into there; Adrian was wise to stop now. We all got out, and Domnul Cornel went into a nearby small building which turned out to be the local town hall.

A uniformed man came out with a wine bottle and some glasses, and poured us all a glass of wine (Mihaela and Adrian declined politely). It seemed somewhat bizarre to be standing in the rain, our feet deep in the mud, drinking wine with the village policeman. If I had not been so nervous, I would have relished the moment. As it was, I discreetly poured most of my throat-burning drink away when no one was looking and went to stand with Mihaela and Adrian, who were chatting quietly together. This was an area they had never been to before and they were quite enjoying the outing, though, like me, very aware of how much depended on it. The others bade farewell to the hospitable policeman, and we all began to pick our way through the mud towards Emilia's house. There was still quite some distance to go, and the path was very steep. Mihaela, Adrian and I sang songs to keep our spirits up. I suddenly remembered a 'golden oldie' from my youth club days:

I know who holds the future, and he has me in his hand.
With God things don't just happen, everything by him is
    planned.
So as I face tomorrow, with its problems great and small,
I'll trust the God of miracles, give to him my all.

I sang it with all my heart, handing over yet again my uncertain future – and Robert's – to the God of miracles, who loved us.

The rain was getting heavier. As we passed a woodyard, both Nicu and Domnul Cornel picked up bits of wood and held them over their heads as impromptu umbrellas. Finally we arrived at Emilia's dwelling. Nicu and Domnul Cornel went up the steps and knocked on the door. I shivered with nerves and cold, thinking back to the first time I had stood here, waiting for Emilia to appear. She came to the door, holding a baby, looking more worn and tired than I remembered her. This was her second child since Robert, and he was not yet three. No wonder she seemed so exhausted. Her eyes acknowledged me, but she didn't say anything. Nicu opened the discussion, and then it ranged backwards and forwards, sometimes quite vehemently. I tried to follow what was being said, but I couldn't keep up with the speed of the speech. Mihaela was concentrating too hard to translate, and Adrian was actually joining in, using a gentle tone and conciliatory gestures. Emilia glanced at me uncertainly, and I smiled, willing her to soften her attitude. Nicu moved towards me, speaking to Mihaela.

'She says that you promised to get work for her in England, and you did not. That is why she take away the permission.'

'We did not promise. We said that we would find out if it was possible, and we did that. Unfortunately, she cannot come to England to work. We tried to explain this to her in September when Graham was here. We did try, but it is the law.' Privately, I wondered how practical it would have been for Emilia, uneducated and with very young children, to find work in England even if she could have got a permit. The myth of the rich cure-all West would have worn a bit thin after a while.

Emilia shrugged and didn't say anything, so I took the opportunity to try and speak to her myself, appealing to her maternal instinct. Mustering up my best Romanian, I said, 'Robert is not happy in the children's home. He is very sad. I will make him happy in England. I love him.' Despite myself, my voice trembled, and I saw tears in her eyes too. Nicu interjected something, and then, just as it seemed that Emilia was going to change her mind, her partner came up the steps and started shouting at Domnul Cornel and Nicu. He was aggressive in his stance and speech, and my heart sank.

Emilia looked at me and pointed towards the door behind her, asking if I would like to come in. Touched by this gesture, I smiled and thanked her, following her into the most poverty-stricken home I have ever been in. It consisted of two rooms. I was standing in the living area, which was small and squalid. The floor was filthy, strewn with food, mud and animal droppings, as were the few pieces of furniture. On the table stood a naked little girl of about two. She was standing in a puddle of urine, right next to a lump of raw meat. Flies were buzzing round the table and the floor, and settling on the meat. A wave of revulsion swept through me, but that was followed by a deep sadness and compassion for the people who had to live in such conditions. I reached out and touched the little girl, greeting her in Romanian, and then took out one of the toys I had brought. She stood holding it for ages, looking at it in wonder. I gave a soft toy to the baby, and asked the children's names: Lunita and Ioana, Robert's half-sisters, children he would probably never meet. Mihaela called me from outside, perhaps worried by my disappearance. I went out, glad of the fresh air, and joined her.

Nicu, Adrian and Emilia's man were still in animated discussion. Domnul Cornel, meanwhile, was poking round the back of the house, making notes as he went. Spotting Emilia, he went over to her and started asking questions. A little different from the months of intensive questioning we had undergone for our home study! But Domnul Cornel was taking everything in. He went inside the house, and emerged some time later with a look of distaste on his face. Emilia's man, who, Mihaela informed me, was called Radu, nodded to the others and went up to Emilia. They began talking rapidly, debating various points. Emilia seemed to be holding her ground. Finally, she spoke to Nicu, who had been hovering nearby. He replied and looked pleased.

Everyone began to make a move towards the track, saying goodbye to the couple on the steps. My eyes met Emilia's and I tried to read her thoughts. But it was impossible to fathom that enigmatic gaze. I called '*la revedere*' and turned away. We squelched down the track in silence, though I was eager to know exactly what was happening. Once again, I felt the frustration of not being able to influence events at all. Things had been said today that would have a profound effect down the years on me and my family, and I couldn't even understand what they were. I had to trust others to speak and act for me. I decided that this was a humbling experience, and probably very good for me!

We reached the car, and Mihaela said, 'Emilia has agreed to come to the court next week for an adoption hearing. We said that you would pay the bus fare.'

'Oh, of course,' I agreed, light-headed with relief. Surely she would cancel her withdrawal now, and give her consent to the adoption? 'Isn't that good, that she has agreed to come?'

'If she *does* come,' said Mihaela gloomily. But I refused to be discouraged. It had been an emotionally draining day, and I was too tired to consider any more possibilities.

It seemed an age to wait for the adoption hearing, but I spent a good deal of the intervening time in the orphanage, wanting to be with Robert as much as possible. I was developing good relationships with the asistente. They appreciated my help, and the fact that I did not concentrate exclusively on Robert but lent a hand wherever it was needed. I was not afraid to get myself dirty (and frequently did) and I must have made their job easier at times when the aid workers were not there. They laughed at my frequent mistakes in Romanian, but nonetheless encouraged me to keep trying. One of them once told me, when I was apologising for not being able to talk to her properly, that the carers all admired me for at least trying to communicate with them. They seemed to resent the presence of the English girls, complaining that they only ever spoke to them through Leah, the interpreter.

I could sympathise with both sides. The girls were only coming out for a short time, often using precious holiday to do so, and the shock of conditions in the orphanage made them desperate to create change and improve the lives of the children. But the carers, many of whom lived in near-poverty themselves, felt misunderstood and devalued by these young people who came from comfortable lifestyles and started telling them what to do, with no real understanding of their context or culture. As with all aid situations throughout world history, the problem was to strike a sensitive balance between helping those in need and imposing, rather than nurturing, an alternative system.

I had expected some hostility from the Romanian workers because I wished to take a child out of the country, but in fact they all seemed supportive, as well as amazed that I wanted another child when I already had four. We agreed that Ceausescu would have been proud of me for keeping to the required five offspring! Several of them, though, questioned why it was Robert that I was adopting, implying that there were others who would be a better choice. I was actually challenged more about the adoption by an English girl working in the orphanage, who held to the ideological stance that it is morally wrong to take a child away from its culture and heritage. While I agreed with that in principle and would never have adopted from a family, I argued that the culture of the orphanage and the mental asylum was not one that any child should have to live in. The long-term strategy must be to change the fundamental attitude towards the disadvantaged in Romania, but any change in the system would come too late for Robert and his peers.

One of the asistente, Ana, was especially friendly towards me, and always made a point of speaking to me and trying to help in whatever way she could. One day, she invited me to visit her at her apartment before her shift at the orphanage. I was touched by the invitation, and arranged to meet her at the market in the older part of the town. I was able to find my way round quite well now. All those walks with Elizabeth last Christmas were paying off! Often, after I had been to the orphanage, I would walk back a different way, exploring other areas of the town.

There was a such a mix of traditional and modern. I guessed that the community had originally been little more than a rural market centre, before the Communist regime had added concrete blocks of flats and offices and grey uniform shops with no goods to put in them. There was a certain amount of industry now around the periphery, and the area was famous for its porcelain. Interspersed among the apartment blocks and terraces were old houses in pastel peaches, greens and greys, with steeply sloping roofs and small turrets, still with their own land and smallholdings. It was not unusual to come across a pig snuffling along the fence as you walked by, or to hear the persistent crow of a cockerel. Rodica's parents owned such a house, and the land around it was planted with vegetables and sunflowers, with a hen coop in one corner and a pig pen in another. The dog slept in a kennel near the gate. Some of the houses I saw were very big, and looked as if, in their heyday, they would have been extremely gracious and elegant. Now they seemed rather unkempt and shabby, like the faded beauty of a weary old lady.

I got to our arranged meeting place, Piata Cetate, in good time, and wandered round the market stalls, enjoying the bustling noisy atmosphere. The main goods on sale were cabbages, of varying sizes and colours, and practically every stall was selling them and nothing else. I wondered how all the stall holders managed to make a living. Did everyone charge the same? And would all the cabbages sell? While pondering these questions, I caught sight of Ana buying a cabbage, and hurried over to greet her. She was very pleased to see me. I expect, like me, she had wondered whether we had both understood the arrangements for meeting. We crossed the road to a sidestreet and went through a maze of other streets until we reached her apartment block.

Ana, like most Romanians I had met, was very hospitable. She insisted on giving me a meal, despite my protestations, and started heating up a nameless stew which was already in a pan on the stove. It was 10.30 a.m. and I had not long had breakfast, but I realised that to refuse would be to cause offence. However, I had to draw the line when she got out an unlabelled, obviously home-brewed bottle of *tsuica*, remembering Graham's breakfast encounter with a similar bottle in Cimpeni. Ana took absolutely no notice of my polite but firm refusal and my explanation that it was too early, I was not used to strong drink, and so on, and pressed a glass on me. 'It is the custom of friends,' she said (I think!). Raising my glass to her, I took a cautious sip. My whole mouth caught fire immediately, and I choked as I swallowed. My throat felt as if it had swollen right up, and tears started from my eyes. Ana laughed in delight. 'Good?' she said in English. 'Good,' I gasped, smiling at her.

The presence of the English aid workers from Project Alba was a great comfort to me. They were always so friendly and sympathetic, and it was such a relief to be able to speak my own language. Even one's sense of humour can have a subtly racial – not racist – flavour, and it was marvellous to be on the same wavelength as these girls. Once again I realised how important laughter and humour were as a safety valve for all the emotional and spiritual demands we were undergoing. One day I was amazed to meet someone I actually recognised from York. Karen was a nursery nurse who had worked in the York Hospital playroom. I had met her when leaving my children there so that I could go to an appointment or visit friends who were patients. How strange to meet her now in the middle of Romania!

The aid workers all worked extremely hard, mostly dividing their time between the orphanage and the hospital. In the latter, there were actual nursing or auxiliary tasks to do, but in the orphanage it was more a matter of playing with the children and helping to socialise them. There was an official Romanian 'educator' now, Diana, but I never saw her doing much other than chatting to the asistente, doing her elegant nails or smoking on the balcony. The aid workers really tried to teach the children how to play with toys and how to share with each other and take turns in games. It was an uphill task, for the techniques and strategies were not practised when the workers were not there.

The children went mad when toys were introduced, pushing and fighting to grab something, and then holding on to it with a grasp of iron. The orphanage grip, we called it. Not only that, but they then raced round, trying to snatch the toys from each other. The shrieks and wails were deafening. If we did succeed in sitting a few of them down and showing them how a toy worked or how it could be played with, we were soon disrupted by others, who dived in to grab the toy or jump on us. In fact, adults who took time to relate to the children were the most popular toy of all. We were jumped on, climbed over, pulled, pinched and punched. Being an aid worker was no soft option.

It was heartbreaking to see those children who did not even have sufficient spirit to be aggressive: those who sat and rocked all day, or went on their hands and knees and banged their heads rhythmically against the wall, those who curled up in a foetal position and would not move, and those who spent most of their time crying. It was almost impossible to get through to them, but also impossible not to keep trying.

The Project Alba workers stayed, on average, two or three weeks, though some were able to stay for longer and there was one paid co-ordinator who was based out there. Sometimes, they felt as if all they did was futile, in the face of the huge changes that were needed in the system, but I was sure that they had made a significant difference to the young lives they had cared for. The love and attention the children had received, though it was comparatively brief, would remain with them as a valuable deposit in the years to come. The aid workers were also acting as role models for the Romanian workers, showing them an alternative, more caring way of looking after the children.

I was invited round for supper one evening, and gladly accepted. The charity owned or rented an apartment quite near to where I was living, and though not very big for the number staying there it was a haven from the difficulties of their work and daily life in general. Everyone who came out brought supplies from home, so they were quite well stocked with chocolate, packet soups, biscuits and other little extras to help life flow more smoothly. We had a super time together, interspersing joking and banter with more serious exchanges of views and information. Though I was late back, I felt quite refreshed by my evening out.

My visits to the Casa de Copii continued to be difficult and at times traumatic experiences. The children were so damaged and distressed. The orphanage followed a strict routine, and I used to come at different times and join in whatever activity was happening. They stayed in their cots for a large part of the morning, while they were changed out of their wet or dirty nightwear and toileted. This took quite a long time, and they would then be left in the cots for a further period. Some children would climb out and run around, or get into another cot and start attacking the occupant, but on the whole they remained passively where they had been left. It was what they were used to.

After a while there was a time of free play, *joc liber*. This was when the aid workers laboured most intensively and the asistente stood and watched. It was good that the children were out of their cots and exercising their bodies, but it was evident that most of them found it a very threatening situation to be in. I found it threatening myself at times!

At noon it was lunchtime. The aid workers went off to the hospital, and two carers and I were left to feed twenty-five two-year-olds, many of whom could not chew and most of whom could not feed themselves. All those who could sit unaided were made to sit down at the table. The others, like Robert, were either fed in their cots or put into supported seats.

Often, the asistente would go off to the kitchens to collect the food, leaving me to keep control on my own. It was a scary prospect. In a moment of inspiration one day, I started singing to them and they quietened down immediately. If my friends could see me now, I thought, standing in front of all these Romanian orphans, singing 'Pop Goes the Weasel'. That was their favourite, because of the 'pop', and they asked for it again and again, remembering each day, as soon as they sat down at the table. One of the carers listened to me for a while, and then sang a Romanian song. We smiled at each other, sharing the pleasure.

The food was basic but edible, often a thick soup with a meatball stuck in it, or mashed up vegetables. But much was wasted because the children could not manage to feed themselves, or they spilt or threw it. They usually used their fingers to eat and then wiped their messy hands on their shaven hair, or that of their neighbour. The noise was unbelievable, and many children were most distressed by the whole procedure. I tried to help as many as I could, but it was difficult as I was also feeding Robert. He couldn't swallow very well, and often choked on the slightest lump. The carers constantly shouted at the children to hurry, and took away bowls that were still full, just to speed things up.

At 1.00 p.m. the children were put down for a three-hour rest, having been forced through the toilet area again. They were given a snack at 4.00 p.m. and then allowed to run free again until their evening meal. This was the time when they might be allowed out into the gradina, but only the ones who could walk were taken out. Once, when I came back in for something, I found other children left completely alone. Most of them were lying or standing silently in their cots, staring blankly into space as they rocked slowly backwards and forwards. One child was sitting, immobile, at a table. He was blind. There was nothing for him to feel or do with his hands, and nothing for him to listen to. Completely isolated, he must have been there for at least an hour. I touched his hand, and his small fingers curled round mine, gripping them tightly. My eyes smarted with tears, and I felt a burning lump in my chest. I picked him up and cuddled him, soothing him with words of comfort. He sat quietly, not resisting, but not responding either. I sat him back down and piled lots of toys on the table in front of him, guiding his hands and showing him how to play with them. As I walked back to the gradina and Robert, I felt overwhelmed with helpless frustration. I wanted to help all these children. How could I rescue only one? They all needed to escape from these conditions. Why couldn't I do more?

The children were bathed once a week, on a Tuesday. As soon as the taps began to fill the big stone sink, some of the children began to scream and run away. They recognised the signs that a bath was on the way. The first child was grabbed and undressed and then put struggling in the water. He stood in the sink, shrieking his objections. Greasy evil-smelling soap was applied roughly to the squirming body, and then water splashed all over to remove it. The child was whisked out and given to the other carer, who rubbed him briskly with a towel. The next was stripped and put in the sink. And so it continued. All twenty-five were bathed in the same water, and with very few changes of towel. By the end of the session the water was a murky brown and smelt disgusting. All the children were crying and upset.

I did what I could to help, putting on their nightclothes and trying to comfort them as I did so. At least the hot water was more frequent than in the apartment blocks, but I knew there were times when the children were washed down in cold water. It was not surprising that they so hated having their clothes off. Even when they had dirtied themselves and the mess was slipping down their legs to collect at the feet of their tights, they did not want to be changed, but clung on to their clothes as if to a lifebelt. The children were never properly clean. Their skin was permeated with the smell of the orphanage, and their clothes were grey and stained, even when they had just returned from being washed.

The laundry was situated in the basement, a dark dank room with green walls. It consisted of huge ancient machines which boiled the clothes for hours. Neither the machines nor the washing powder (if they used any) were very efficient; moreover, they had to contend with unusually disgusting clothes. Most of the children in the orphanage were not toilet trained, but only the babies wore nappies. So they regularly dirtied and wet their clothes. I started bringing in my own supply for Robert for night-time use, but did not have enough for days as well. A child who dirtied himself just after a toileting time would have to wait for the next one, three or four hours later, before he was changed. Consequently, the clothes, as well as the child, were in a dreadful state. On several occasions, I went to rinse out the filthy tights before putting them in the laundry pile, but was stopped by the asistente. 'That's not your job,' they said. 'It's for the laundry workers.' I imagined that the clothes were put straight into the machines with all the excrement still attached. Project Alba were raising funds to install a new laundry, with modern machines, and I fervently hoped that they would soon succeed.

With the lack of basic hygiene practice in the orphanage, it was not surprising that there was a great deal of illness among both children and staff. Most of the youngsters had permanently runny noses and coughs, and some of them looked far more seriously ill. The close proximity of the cots to each other and the communal bedding and toilet arrangements meant that germs were quickly passed. One of the first Romanian phrases I learnt was 'Wash your hands!'

One day, I came in to see Diana, the 'educator', injecting herself with difficulty in the thigh. She then handed the syringe to another woman. I was startled. Surely they wouldn't be so overt in doing drugs? And where had they got them from? Diana caught my expression and laughed.

'Vaccine,' she explained, waving at a tray full of small phials and a few syringes. 'For children.'

'Why?' I asked, surprised that the orphanage could keep up an immunisation programme.

'*Hepatit*,' came the answer. Alarmed, I tried to find out more, but it was difficult to understand the explanations so I went in search of the English workers or Leah the interpreter. It turned out that several cases of hepatitis A had been discovered. The rest of the children were being vaccinated as a precaution, although no one knew exactly with what. Gammaglobulin was available in the West as an immunisation against hepatitis A, but we did not think it had reached Romania yet. I hadn't been offered it myself before travelling. We were also very worried about the danger of using shared needles to administer the vaccination. The aid workers were going to take it up with the director.

When I returned to Robert's salon, I noticed that one of the cots contained a very sick child. She was lying still with her eyes closed, and her skin had a pale yellow tinge to it. The next day, there were two more in a similar situation, and one of the babies in another salon was in a serious condition. I redoubled my efforts at keeping everyone clean, particularly before meals, and even brought in some soap to supplement the meagre supply. Hepatitis A, though not as serious as B, is a very nasty virus; it attacks the liver and can leave the victim debilitated for weeks afterwards. It is transmitted mainly through sewage and impure water supplies, which is why hygiene is particularly vital in this context. I worried that Robert would catch it. He was so frail and weak that I feared the virus would affect him badly. The days passed and he seemed fine, but as I knew there was a long incubation period, I was not really pacified. I prayed for him each day, asking for the Lord's protection in every area of his life.

8

A nation in transition

The social report would not be ready until the following week, and the adoption hearing was scheduled for Thursday. That gave me time to pursue some of the other documents which were still required and to spend time with Robert. I was also very much enjoying being part of Romanian life. Living with Romanians rather than in a hotel or with aid workers meant that I had a privileged insight into another culture and way of life.

Just before the Romanian Easter Sunday, when we still had the borrowed car, Adrian, Mihaela and I went down to the market to collect some things for Mihaela's relatives, who lived in a small village just outside Alba. The market was busy, full of people bustling here and there, shouting their wares, disputing prices, passing the time of day. I noticed immediately that there was an additional sound in the usual cacophony: the sound of bleating. Everywhere were small lambs, tethered to stalls, penned in makeshift cages, even peering out of car windows. Here and there, men carried them over their shoulders in true biblical fashion. I realised, with a sinking heart, that this was the logical follow-on from the pigs at Christmas. Was I now going to see lambs slaughtered in the streets? With their cute little faces and pathetic bleat, they tugged at the heartstrings even more than the unfortunate pigs had done.

Adrian couldn't understand my attitude at all, and watched with great perplexity as I stroked a lamb, exclaiming with distress over its plight. To him, animals were a means of sustenance, not beings with feelings. There was no room for such sentimentality in a country that struggled to feed itself. He went over to an area of the market where a tight knot of people stood around. The ground was stained a dark reddish brown, and little rivulets of red liquid trickled down the path near by. Adrian haggled with a stallholder for a while, and then heaved up the carcass of a lamb and came back towards us, laughing at my look of horror. I thought that even carnivores in England would not like to deal with meat like this.

The corpse was dumped in the boot and we set off for Mihaela's grandparents' village. It was like stepping back in time. They lived in a lovely old house in the traditional style of the area. Hens roamed the garden, and a large well provided the only water. It looked very quaint and fairy-tale, but I imagined coming out in the winter, breaking the ice and plunging the bucket down, just to get washed and make a cup of tea. There was no electricity or gas, and a woodstore in one of the outhouses indicated the main source of fuel for the ancient stove in the living-room. An earth closet at the end of the garden was the only sanitation. Life would not be easy in this seemingly idyllic village.

Mihaela's grandparents greeted me warmly and invited us in. The rooms were dark but cosy, the floors and walls covered with vivid rugs in deep lush colours. There were some fine pieces of solid wood furniture, beautifully carved and polished. *Bunica* – Grandma – offered us refreshments, and then showed me some wonderfully decorated eggs. Dyeing hard-boiled eggs and then transferring leaf and flower shapes on to them is a Romanian Easter custom. I exclaimed in delight at their delicate beauty. When it was time to go, she gave me some of the eggs *'pentru copii'* – for the children. I stammered my thanks, quite overwhelmed by this gesture of friendship.

Meanwhile, there seemed to be no progress on the legal side at all. We were still waiting for Domnul Cornel to produce the social report on Emilia, and I needed to complete the procedure to gain entry clearance for Robert to travel to England with me, or he would be an illegal immigrant when

129

we finally arrived at Heathrow. I decided that I would go to Bucharest and see what could be done. Phone calls had not produced much joy so far, so I would try going to the Embassy in person. The thought of a weekend with the Pughs in Bucharest was very attractive. The emotional, mental and physical demands of the past week had left me exhausted, and I knew that I could relax and be myself with Mair, John and the girls.

On the Saturday morning, I called in early at the orphanage to say goodbye to Robert. We went into the gradina on our own, and I sat on a swing and held him close. He was more withdrawn than ever, and made no effort to get off my knee and explore. After a while, he fell asleep in my arms, and I stayed there for some time, swinging gently in the sunlight, enjoying the warmth and the quiet. It seemed a shame to disturb such peace, but I had booked a ticket on the early afternoon train and had to leave him. He was dazed by sleep, and hardly noticed as I put him with the other children and kissed him goodbye.

The train drew in to the Gara de Nord in Bucharest, and I eased myself out of my seat. On the platform, dozens of young men tried to persuade me to travel to Istanbul. I wasn't quite sure why they wanted me to go there in particular, but I shook my head and hurried on. John was waiting in the main concourse and I gave him an affectionate hug, delighted to be back with these friends again. It would be good to have a bit longer with them, instead of using them as a transit hotel. The city was in a state of high excitement, John told me, because the exiled king, Mihai, was returning to the capital tomorrow for the first time since the Communists seized power in 1947. It was not an official visit – he was attending a family wedding – but the Romanians were treating it like one. We all decided that we would like to be part of this historic occasion. That evening we stayed up late, chatting, making plans, catching up with each others' news and generally putting the world to rights.

The next day, we went to the Anglican church in Bucharest, where the Pughs worshipped. It was a strange experience. As soon as I walked through the doors, I felt as if I was back in England — that timeless safe element of England. There was the chime of hushed English voices, the smell of candles and furniture wax, the lovely flower arrangements, the stained glass windows. The church was a focal point for the expatriate community in Bucharest, and embassy officials mixed with itinerant aid workers from various English-speaking countries, and a scattering of business people. There were also quite a few Africans, who had come to the university in Bucharest.

The service was the same as any Anglican service the world over, and gave me a secure feeling, conjuring images of my childhood and the village church where I used to sit and hear these same words before going to Sunday School. It was hard to believe that we were actually in Romania. Even the notices seemed familiar: socials, a coffee morning, the cleaning rota — only a jumble sale was missing. After the service, we had the opportunity to chat over coffee and biscuits. People were friendly and kind, and all had interesting stories as to how they came to be in Romania. It was evident that Mair and John were an important part of church life, and that their openness and hospitality had nurtured many who were lonely or homesick.

We left the church building and joined the busy flow of people making for the city centre. The sun was very hot by now, and I was beginning to wish I had worn something cooler. As we neared our destination the throng grew denser, and we realised that it was going to be very crowded indeed. I speculated that perhaps there had not been such a gathering since the Ceausescus were overthrown in December 1989. We sat down in a grassy area to eat our picnic lunch. We had been joined by Ruth, an older lady who had left her family behind for a period of months to work with the street children of Bucharest.

The charity she was with had a night shelter and tried to

131

feed, clean and care for these children on a regular basis. It sounded very hard work, as the children were often violent or on drugs. They were tough emotionally hardened survivors who didn't trust anyone. Yet Ruth and her colleagues were learning how to reach into their inner hurting selves and give them back some sense of love and self-worth. It was a slow heartbreaking and at times utterly frustrating process but, Ruth told me, they had seen some real breakthroughs.

While we were finishing our lunch and Ionela was enjoying a run round on the grass, I went over to investigate something I had spotted on the way past. Situated on the edge of some flower beds, by the pavement, was a wooden cross, of the design often seen in Orthodox churches. There was an inscription on it, and a candle set at the intersection of the cross. At the foot were a scattering of smaller candles, burning brightly despite the sunlight, and many bunches and posies of fresh flowers. Rebecca had joined me, and she read the inscription.

'It's a memorial to some people who died in this street during the revolution,' she said. I shivered, despite the heat, and looked around at the happy groups of people enjoying a relaxing Sunday afternoon. The air was filled with laughter and children calling to each other. Impossible to believe that, in this very place, men and women had fought each other and died. That here, where the sun shone and families played, there had existed hatred and desperation, and a grim determination to overcome the forces of evil that had gripped the country for so long. Yet it had happened, only two and a half years ago, and the scars of the nation were still very raw. It was hard to imagine living in a country which had undergone such a violent political upheaval so recently. I reflected that for all the tabloid scaremongering and the many political and social problems, Britain was actually in a very stable state. I didn't feel complacent, but thankful that we had not had to undergo such internal pain.

There was a general move towards the city centre. Someone

obviously knew when King Mihai was due to appear. As we approached Piata Universitate, we could hear a triumphant chant – '*Regele Mihai, Regele Mihai!*' My skin prickled with excitement in the emotionally charged atmosphere. The crowd had swelled to thousands but there was no sense of threat or danger: everyone seemed happy and excited rather than angry. Many people were carrying flowers and pictures of Mihai, and everywhere the chant continued. We came to a stop; it was impossible to move any further for the press of people. Determined to get a photograph of this amazing occasion, I climbed on to a bollard and stood, wobbling precariously, trying to keep my balance while focusing my camera. Behind me, John had joined others on top of a big road sign.

The sight through my camera lens took my breath away. The entire square was crammed with noisy rejoicing people, and every road leading into the square was similarly filled: an enormous slow-moving river of humanity, coming to honour the king.

Suddenly, there was a stirring at one side of the square and the chanting rose to a roar. Everyone surged forward and I was nearly swept off my bollard. '*Vine rege!*' – the king is coming! – went round the crowds, and we all craned our necks for a view. Down one side of the Piata, a way was being cleared through the throng, and some people were walking along it, followed by a car. I could only see the tops of heads and an occasional flash of the car, but the people nearest were waving enthusiastically to the king, hoisting their placards and photos high in the air, and the cheers reached an amazing crescendo as he passed. Apparently he was going to a building much further down the street, where he would make an appearance on the balcony. It would be impossible for us to get there because of the volume of people all trying to reach the same place. I climbed carefully down from the bollard, and smiled at a man who was standing near me. His eyes were full of tears.

'This is a wonderful day for Romania,' he said. 'The king has come back.' I was moved by the depth of his emotion, and noticed that many others were also in tears. I asked the man if he thought that King Mihai would come back to Romania permanently. 'That is our hope,' he said, 'the only hope for Romania.' I remembered the man Elizabeth and I had talked to for so long in the frozen train. We had dubbed him Mihai the monarchist, because he and his friends were so convinced that the only way forward constitutionally for Romania was through the monarchy. Judging by today's turnout, he was by no means alone in his conviction.

Exhausted by the heat and the excitement, we made our way back to where we had left the car, and went home for a drink and a rest. Later, taking Ruth to work, we stopped to visit an important monument to Romania's recent history, the Cemetery of the Revolution. It was a peaceful sombre place, comprising row upon row of white marble tombstones. I was struck immediately by how many there were. They stretched away in every direction, a potent reminder of the cost of revolution. Each tombstone had a photograph on it, as well as an inscription detailing the victim's name, background and manner of life and death. The photographs brought home very graphically how young these people were when they died defending their beliefs. Some of them had been little more than children, thirteen- and fourteen-year-olds, caught up in a battle they did not initiate or understand. There were many in their late teens and twenties, no doubt fired with the idealism of youth to throw off something they believed was inherently wrong.

As I wandered along the rows, pausing to gaze at photo-graphs and make out the inscriptions, I tried to imagine the people behind them, their hopes and fears, their daily lives, all brought to a halt by a violent episode in history which happened to affect them. I was saddened by the loss of life, yet inspired by their bravery and determination. Would they consider now that their deaths had made a difference, I mused, or would they feel that they had died in vain? I had spoken to many Romanians who, despite acknowledging that there had been improvements in life since the revolution, believed that nothing had changed fundamentally. The same people were in government, merely giving themselves a new name; until they lost power, Romania could not make true progress. The President, Iliescu, one of Ceausescu's ministers in the old regime, was deeply unpopular with many. In fact, a story was doing the rounds that the Chinese thought the Romanian President's first name was Jos, because they had seen so many television pictures of walls daubed with *Jos Iliescu*. *Jos* actually means 'down with'! The transition from Communist dictatorship to modern market economy was a long and difficult one. For the ordinary people, abstract gains like freedom and democracy were insignificant compared to the fact that the price of bread rose every week. They were beginning to think that things had been better in the old days.

We dropped Ruth at the night shelter, an old house with a back yard surrounded by a high fence. Children were already beginning to congregate there as we arrived, some of them yelling, scrapping and racing around, others just huddled up against the fence, their faces blank. Their clothes were torn and dirty and their hair was matted. They all crowded round Ruth as she got out, gesticulating and asking questions, but she shook her head, laughing, pointed to her watch and went into the house alone.

Rather than go straight back to the apartment, John suggested that we go to a nearby park, for a walk and to let the children play on the swings and slides. The evening had an almost balmy feel, and it was good to relax and enjoy the warmth. Ionela, Hannah and Rebecca had a wonderful time in the playground. As I sat and watched them, I realised how important it was for me to see normal Romanian families involved in normal family activities. I had become so used to seeing damaged, deprived, suffering children that I was in danger of developing a distorted view of the social situation. Here in the busy playground were many youngsters enjoying themselves with their parents, just as they would in England or anywhere else. People here didn't have all the luxuries and privilege that we so often took for granted in the West, but basically they were the same, with the same feelings, ambitions and hopes. The majority of children in Romania lived happy cared-for lives within a family structure, and grew up to be law-abiding citizens. I watched as children screamed with delight on the swings and dads played football with their sons, and a sense of right proportion returned to me.

The next day, John dropped me off at the end of the Embassy's road on his way to work. The building, set in its own grounds behind a high fence, was grand and elegant, the remnant of a more gracious age. I showed my passport to the sentry at the gate and was directed to a side door. Once inside the electronically locked doors, I felt as if I'd stepped into another world. The entrance lobby was spacious, with chairs and low tables dotted about for those waiting for appointments. High ceilings and pastel-coloured walls made the rooms light and airy, and my feet trod on plush carpet. The air of opulence provided a striking contrast to the poverty just outside the gates. I remembered Mair saying that certain foodstuffs and other items unavailable in Romania were specially shipped in for the staff. I wondered if they found it a problem of conscience to live so luxuriously in a country that was struggling to feed itself, or whether the expatriate lifestyle was so cocooned that the question did not arise.

In the office, I asked to see Ms Hitchens. While the receptionist rang through for me, I waited in the lobby, too interested in the comings and goings to read the glossy magazines on the table. At length, Ms Hitchens arrived, a short dark-haired lady who looked quite weary. She was businesslike but friendly, and didn't sound nearly as negative as she had on the phone. I explained the urgency of the situation and my need to get home to my family, and she promised to try and speed things up. They had received the medical but not the social report, and were also waiting for some sort of confirmation as to our status from the Department of Health.

It suddenly occurred to me that the consent to the adoption, which we had filed with the Embassy in May the previous year and which formed the basis of our application for an entry visa, was no longer valid. Obviously, when Emilia withdrew her consent in the court at Alba Iulia, neither the Embassy nor the Committee had been informed. I breathed a sigh of relief when Ms Hitchens didn't mention it. Emilia would surely cancel her withdrawal next week, so there was no need to start up the bureaucratic machine again unnecessarily. Reluctantly accepting that I was not going to walk out of the Embassy with an entry visa for Robert, I pleaded again the urgency of my case, then thanked her and came away. As I reviewed our conversation, I realised that the official had still spoken in terms of obtaining the visa *before* being able to have an adoption hearing. I was puzzled, because the court had not made it a requirement as long as the visa had been applied for. I decided that I would stick with the court's ruling, since they had the sway of law, and wouldn't rock the boat with further complications.

I walked back to the Pughs' apartment through the busy dirty streets, enjoying the atmosphere of the metropolis. The shops were better stocked than in Alba Iulia, though to a poor standard compared to the West. There was no concept of window displays and very little advertising. Goods were set out in a utilitarian manner, in piles on the floor or stacked in boxes on the shelves. There were not many prices shown, perhaps because they kept changing so often. If you did venture into a shop, the unsmiling assistant served you with a few curt words or else ignored you altogether. Add to that the system of queuing in each shop, sometimes to get a ticket, sometimes to buy an item, and shopping Romanian-style was quite an un-nerving experience.

I passed a gypsy woman sitting on the pavement with her baby wrapped up beside her. The woman's head was covered in a bright headscarf, and she was wearing a traditional floral skirt. Her face was worn and wizened beyond her years as, ignored and isolated, she called out to passers-by. The dilemma of street beggars is by no means unique to Romania, but there seemed to be so very many in Bucharest. Impulsively, I went into a nearby bakery and brought her some bread and cake. It was only a very short-term solution, but I didn't know what else to do. There was no social security or housing benefit for these poor people to claim: no giros or hostels, nothing. At the bottom of the social scale, they were treated as misfits and outcasts, with no welfare state to give them even a little support. What future did that baby have? Probably it would end up in one of Bucharest's infamous orphanages, or as a street child, sleeping in the sewers and heating vents under the Gara de Nord, and begging and stealing to survive. Guilty and frustrated, I hurried on, my enjoyment of the walk spoiled by what I had seen.

On the way back, I stopped at a post office and managed to put a call through to England. Graham and I had been able to talk a few times but I hadn't spoken to the boys for ages and had now been away from them for nearly two weeks. My mother answered the phone. She had come up from Berkshire to look after the children, so that Graham could go back to work. It was so good to know that she was there with them, supplying some stability to the family. The excitement of Grandma's visit would more than compensate for Mummy being away! Although Mum had some doubts about the wisdom of adopting Robert, she had always supported us practically, and I was so grateful to her for giving up time and effort to be with the children now. I chatted cheerfully to each of the boys in turn, listening to their bits of news and telling them how much I loved them. Afterwards, I put the phone down over-whelmed by homesickness and the desire to be with my family.

Back at the Pughs' apartment, the girls were surrounded by clothes and bags. Ionela was rushing round with various items of clothing, shouting 'Holiday! Holiday!' Mair smiled at my bemused expression and explained that they had decided to take a few days off and come to Alba Iulia on the train with me. I was absolutely delighted.

'Oh, that's wonderful! You'll meet Robert, and be there for the hearing, and I can show you the town, and the mountains are so near . . .'

They were laughing as I ran out of breath, but they were as excited as I was. Just to have them near would be a wonderful support in what promised to be a difficult week.

I glanced at the clothes on the beds. 'So how long are you coming up for?'

'Oh, only a couple of days,' replied Mair, 'John can't have any longer off work. Why?'

'The girls have got enough clothes out for a couple of weeks,' I teased.

'Oh, we're not taking them all,' said Rebecca. 'It's just that we can't decide what to take.' I couldn't imagine my boys having that sort of problem; they would just grab the first few things that fell out of the cupboard!

The decisions had to be delayed, however, as John arrived back from work and we all went out to tea with an American missionary couple, Rodney and Carol. They made me very welcome, and again it was good to be able to relax and not worry about being misinterpreted or misunderstood. Rodney and Carol had been in the country some years, having been sent out by their church to work with the equivalent de-nomination in Romania. They did much pastoral work as well as preaching, and seemed happy to be there. Rodney was a likeable man, cheerful and sincere, with a caring heart and a good sense of humour. They put up with the radical change in lifestyle without complaint, and had made their small apartment very homely.

I described my many gaffes in the language, and he told us about a wonderful mistake he had made. He had worked hard to learn Romanian, and wanted to preach in the language rather than use an interpreter. So he embarked on a sermon about the joy of the Lord, and thought he was doing pretty well until he noticed that his congregation were unusually restless; he even saw some smiles and giggles. This is unheard of in Romanian churches, so he began to wonder if something about his appearance was irresistibly funny. After the service, he asked someone what the amusement was about. 'Well,' came the reply, you used the word *bucatarie* all the way through your sermon, instead of *bucurie*.' Rodney had inadvertently preached on the kitchen of the Lord! After that, he went back to using an interpreter.

The next morning, despite the girls' preparations the previous day, no one seemed ready to go. Rebecca and I went down to the station and bought the tickets. Back at the apartment, it was nearly time to leave and John still hadn't had a shower. He insisted that there was plenty of time and told us to go on ahead, since we needed two taxis to get there anyway. The train was in, and Mair, Rebecca and I waited anxiously for the others to appear. The whistle blew, and they had still not arrived.

'You'd better get on,' said Mair, 'You've *got* to get back. It doesn't matter so much about us.'

'Why don't we catch the next one?' I asked, not wanting to go without them.

'It doesn't work like that here – we haven't got the right tickets,' she said. 'Go on, you'll have to go without us.' She was practically in tears of frustration. I leapt on the train as it started to move. As it gathered speed, I saw John, Hannah and Ionela race on to the platform. At the same time, I realised that Mair had kept the picnic lunch, and that I was marooned on the train for the next six or seven hours with nothing to eat or drink.

The time passed better than I expected, chatting to an American working in Bucharest and a Romanian medical student. They both got off at Brasov, and persuaded me to run up the platform there to the first section of the train where there might be a restaurant car. There was, and I managed to get some bread and a drink before running back down the platform at the next stop. Unlike British trains, there was no corridor running the length of the train. When we pulled up at last in Alba Iulia, I was right opposite the exit, and so got to the taxis ahead of the rush. Mihaela and Adrian's flat felt like home, and I was glad to be back. We had a meal and were sitting around exchanging news when the phone rang. Mihaela handed it to me.

'Hi, Sue, it's Mair,' said a cheery voice. 'We're at the Hotel Cetate.'

'You can't be. I've only just got in myself.'

'We know! We followed the train all the way up in the car, and must have missed you by minutes at goodness knows how many stations – Sinaia, Brasov, Sibiu – and then we were waiting when it got into Alba Iulia, but couldn't see you.' I was amazed and very, very pleased that they had made it after all.

'I'll come round now!' I said excitedly. Mihaela and Adrian looked confused, as they were not used to such spontaneous comings and goings, but despite this Mihaela decided to come with me. She was very shy at the thought of meeting Mair and John, but wouldn't let me walk around at night on my own. I assured her that I knew the way, that I was old enough to look after myself and that she could meet Mair and John tomorrow if she preferred, but she ignored my protestations. I think they felt that their duty of hospitality extended to all areas. Such care dispelled any irritation I might have felt at being fussed over.

In the event, as might be expected, Mihaela got on very

well with the Pughs, and we had an enjoyable evening together. The hotel was in the old fortressed part of the town, up the hill from the orphanage. We arranged that the family would come down there the next day, though we doubted that they would actually be allowed inside.

I was on my way early the following morning, eager to see Robert again. I wondered if he would recognise me. On the way I met Nicu, who told me that the social report was still not forthcoming but he was trying to hurry Domnul Cornel along. At the orphanage, the staff were getting the children ready for a little outing to the local playground. Delighted, I hurried off to the Hotel Cetate, to see if the Pughs wanted to come earlier than arranged. We drove down, and I went into the orphanage again, after showing Mair and John where the park was. The children caused some interest as they walked through the streets in a ragged crocodile. I guessed that the inmates of Leagunul Nr 1 were not seen out in public very much. Could this be evidence of a new openness on the part of those in authority?

The playground was not very exciting: a few rusting swings, a broken see-saw, a heavy muddy roundabout and an iron fence which served as a climbing frame. The children didn't seem to mind. Most of them were pleased to be out, and ran round the grassy area screaming and yelling with pleasure. But some of the children, Robert among them, found this new stimulus overwhelming, and stood in the middle of the playground, rocking backwards and forwards, frightened to be outside the security of their familiar environment. I sat down on a slimy bench and put Robert on my knee, with two little girls cuddling up to me as well. We watched the bolder children climbing on the play equipment, and then I saw Mair, John and the girls approaching. Ionela immediately ran to a swing, but the others clustered round to say hello to Robert. The two worlds of inside and outside the orphanage were beginning to converge. He smiled at them, and then wriggled off my knee and walked unsteadily towards Ionela. They stood looking at each other for a while, and then Ionela took his hand and they went off together. It was a lovely sight, and somehow symbolised hope for the future for both of them.

By the time the children returned to the orphanage, it was their lunchtime. I left them to it and went to have a drink and a snack with Mair and John. We wandered round the shops for a while, looking for some cooler clothes for me. I had not brought very much with me, thinking I was only going to be here for a week, and not realising how hot it was in Romania I had brought nearly all winter clothes. It didn't take very long to explore the sartorial possibilities of Alba Iulia, and I just couldn't imagine myself in most of them. The clothes were very poorly made in skimpy cheap fabrics which would not wash very well. The styles were about twenty years out of date, and were either drab and dowdy or with loud psychedelic patterns. However, Rebecca and Hannah found an acceptable divided skirt, with a pretty short-sleeved white blouse to match, in Unirea, one of the town's two department stores. Together they cost the equivalent of three pounds! Such a huge bargain spurred me on to hunt further, and I found some nice shorts and T-shirts for the boys; we spent ages trying to decide sizes. I bought some for Robert, too, ready for when I finally brought him out of the orphanage.

The Pughs decided to go for a drive into the countryside. I wanted to sort out some things at the flat and then see Robert again, so we went our separate ways, agreeing to meet up later in the evening. Back at the apartment, Mihaela and I were having a cup of tea together when the phone rang. It was Nicu, and I could tell that the news was not good. Mihaela was expressing dismay, and days of the week were being mentioned. As usual, I couldn't keep up with the speed of the conversation.

She put the phone down, and told me flatly, 'Mr Cornel say he cannot do social report until next Tuesday, so the adoption trial cannot be until next Wednesday.'

'Next *Wednesday*?' I shouted. 'But that's a whole week away.

I can't wait that long. Surely he can do the report before then?'
I had been relying on all the legal proceedings being completed
at the hearing the next day, so that I could be in England with
Robert by the weekend. The prospect of another week's delay
felt unbearable. How would the children cope for that long
without me? I was desperate to see them and Graham again.
Perhaps I should go back to England for a week and come
back next Tuesday evening.

Mihaela seemed alarmed when I voiced this suggestion, and
said she didn't think it was a good idea. I wasn't sure what her
objection was; there was nothing more to be done here that
required my presence and my children needed me. She shook
her head and told me to speak to Nicu. So I rang him up, and
we struggled to communicate in a stilted mixture of Romanian
and English. He said that he was trying to get hold of Emilia,
to tell her not to come the next day, but that he had so far been
unable to get through to Horea. Obviously Emilia herself was
not on the phone, but he was hoping to leave a message at the
mayor's office. Domnul Cornel's excuse about the social report
was that it had to be signed by some committee which did not
meet again until next Tuesday. I was deeply sceptical, but
powerless. It was evident that Nicu had done what he could to
put pressure on the Municipal Prefect, but without success.

Nicu was strongly against me going back to England. He
gave me the impression that if I went back the adoption hearing
might never happen. I didn't understand, but had been in
Romania long enough to realise that one needed to be forcefully present to get things done. Reluctantly, I abandoned the
idea of flying back, comforting myself with the fact that it
would have been very expensive. I tried to ring home, and then
Elizabeth, but no one answered. Misery wrapped round me
like a blanket. This latest delay, with its reminder that nothing
was assured, that I might still lose Robert, was the last straw. I
felt as if I had lost my will to fight. Yet as I walked down to the
orphanage to visit Robert, I was suddenly aware again of God's

promise and his peace. He had called us to this, and he would not fail us. I did not need to fret, as it said in the psalm Adrian had shared with me, because God was still in control. All I needed to do was to 'wait patiently' – not an easy task for me! – and he surely would 'uphold the justice of my cause'.

9

The law observed

The walk up to the old part of the town was soothing after the noise and smell of the orphanage. Stretched out below were the twinkling lights of the town and outlying villages, each representing households and families with their joys and challenges, hopes and fears. And over everything, the watchful loving eye of God, intimately concerned with all those lives, whether they knew it or not. Awestruck, I continued on my way to the Hotel Cetate.

I had enjoyed myself earlier, playing with my son. He was more lively and alert than I had ever seen him, and we had played a game of peek-a-boo, which he loved. It was supper-time, and he ate with enthusiasm, another small sign of progress. Among all the frustrations and uncertainties, God seemed to be showing me that everything was going to plan after all. I had put Robert to bed quickly, explaining to the asistente that I couldn't help with the other children tonight as I had friends staying.

The hotel stood at the corner of the public gardens which stretch away from the town's Orthodox cathedral. It was a concrete tower block, with a grander than normal entrance and a pleasant if rather gloomy reception area. Altogether, it was of a higher standard than the hotel Graham and I had stayed in (not difficult) but still probably wouldn't have passed health and safety regulations in Britain. However, it was adequate and cheap, so the Pughs were not complaining. They too had been in worse.

Mair and John were upset to hear about the delay in the adoption proceedings, and inclined to agree with me that there was something sinister in Domnul Cornel's refusal to publish

146

the social report. Was he in league with Emilia and her man? Perhaps the Adoption Committee had changed its mind. Could the British Embassy have intervened? Our hypotheses got wilder as the evening wore on, until we were convinced that it was some Communist plot, masterminded by exiled relatives of Ceausescu, to expose foreigners, cause an international incident and so overthrow the government. At this point, I decided it was time to go home! I had to be at the law courts early the next day, as we were still expecting Emilia to arrive for the final adoption hearing. If she did turn up tomorrow, which was by no means certain, how would she react to the news that it had been postponed? Would she be persuaded to come back another day? The questions circled round my head like a pack of wolves about to attack.

The Judecatorie were as busy as ever, even though it was only 8.30 a.m. I had spent so long here, waiting for Nicu, for documents, for Domnul Cornel, that I had become accustomed to the noise and apparent chaos. I still found the acrid pall of cigarette smoke difficult to cope with, though. It seeped into clothes, hair, bags and lungs, and lingered on in nooks and crannies for ages. Emilia wasn't there when we arrived, but that was hardly surprising since her journey was a long one. Mihaela, Adrian and I went from door to door of the various courtrooms, looking at the lists of the day's proceedings, just in case ours had got through after all.

What astonished me was that the vast majority of the cases were petitions for divorce. There must have been hundreds on that day in that court alone. I wondered if it was representative of the country as a whole. Mihaela told me that divorce was very prevalent now; as the Communists had undermined the social and moral framework of the nation, there were no terms of reference for marriage, parenting or citizenship. I reflected sadly that we could see the same trend occurring in Britain, though not yet to the extremes that an oppressive regime had created in Romania.

Nicu appeared, looking harassed, and explained that he was still trying to achieve an adoption hearing that day. He looked even more worried when he realised that Emilia had not arrived, and hurried off. Not long afterwards, Adrian gave an exclamation and nodded to the entrance. There stood Emilia, a little bewildered, with her partner, Radu. We went over, and shook hands. It was an awkward situation, but I was much encouraged by the fact that they had come, especially when I discovered that they had had to get up at 4.00 a.m. in order to catch the right buses. We tried to chat, but everyone was too tense for small talk, and the language barrier simply made matters worse.

Just then, Nicu came back. After greeting Emilia and Radu, he told us privately that Domnul Cornel was still refusing to release the social report until it had been signed by the proper authorities, so the court would not hear the case that day. However, he was going to try and persuade Emilia to sign a document giving consent to our adoption of Robert and cancelling her previous withdrawal of consent in March. If she did this, then she wouldn't need to be present at the adoption hearing the next week, and her journey today would not have been wasted. I held my breath as he explained the situation to Emilia and Radu. It would be the ideal solution if she agreed. Her signed document would be lodged in court with the other papers pertaining to the adoption, and would be legally binding.

After some discussion and questions, Emilia nodded her head. She and the lawyer began to move towards the stairs, while Radu lit up another cigarette and went outside. Hardly daring to believe this turn of events, Adrian, Mihaela and I followed up two flights of stairs to the offices of the judges and the Court President. Nicu knocked on the President's door, and then he and Emilia went inside. It was quiet on this corridor, quite unlike the rest of the building. I could hear the clatter of typewriters from the secretaries' office and a low murmur of voices, but otherwise it was undisturbed, with no running or shouting or hustling crowds of people. We waited outside for what seemed a long time. Then the door opened abruptly, and Emilia burst out and rushed down the corridor in tears. She was immediately followed by Nicu, who hurried after her, calling for her to come back. We looked at each other in amazement and some trepidation, and retraced our steps down the stairs. There was no sign of Emilia or Nicu, so we went outside.

They were standing on the pavement, talking earnestly. Radu had joined them, and he looked angry. I shivered. He would be a frightening man to cross. Mihaela and I hung back, but Adrian went up to them and soon beckoned us over.

'They are going now,' he said. 'Can you give bus fare as agreed?' I handed over the fare and shook hands again, with no idea what was going on. Nicu finished his conversation with Emilia, gave us all a bow and went back into the law courts. Emilia and Radu walked away, and we were left on the pavement wondering what had happened.

'I think,' said Adrian, 'that the President was strict with her. He want to know why she give consent, then take it away, then give it again. He say she do it because she wants money. That is against the law. She didn't like that.'

'But did she sign?' I asked.

He shook his head. 'No.'

'Oh no! What's going to happen now? She'll never give her consent after this.' I was upset. We had been so close to obtaining that vital signature. Adrian, however, was comforting.

'She tell lawyer she will come back next week. She must show President that she didn't want money.' I could see the logic in that. If Emilia didn't sign the consent now, it would point to her demanding money, and she might be prosecuted even though she hadn't actually received any payment. If she did sign, it would prove that she had only the good of the child at heart. It was a complicated situation, and I was not convinced that Emilia's motives were wholly altruistic, though she had seemed moved when I had spoken to her in Horea.

Adrian had to go back to work and Mihaela needed to do some shopping; I decided to go to the orphanage to see Robert. I hadn't been there very long when one of the carers came and asked me to take Robert down to the director's office. Puzzled, I picked him up and went downstairs. As I walked into the room, I stopped abruptly. Emilia was sitting there, waiting to see Robert. She looked almost as surprised to see me as I was to see her, but it was I who was at a disadvantage. She was officially and legally still his mother, even though she had seen him only once or twice in the last two and a half years. She had the legal right to visit him – and to take him away, if she so chose.

I flushed with embarrassment and dismay, feeling myself to be in an intolerable situation, as if I was trying to kidnap the child. With a muttered apology, I thrust Robert at her and fled from the room, leaving him sitting stiffly on her knee. Back in the salon, I was overcome by the emotion of the past few hours. To be the one to hand him back to his natural mother seemed too hard to bear. Perhaps her maternal instincts had been re-awakened by the immediate prospect of adoption, and she had come to take him away. If that was the case then I would not oppose it, as he had a right to live with his natural parents. But it would break my heart to lose him, especially since I had seen where he would be living and could imagine the sort of life he would lead. All the tension and uncertainty found a release as I sobbed over Julie, one of the English aid workers.

Just as I was drying my tears and feeling that I had made rather a fool of myself, Robert was brought back and given to me, and I started crying all over again. He was back, clutching a bar of chocolate which he couldn't eat, and I hugged him close, not wanting to let him go. He touched my wet cheeks and examined his fingers with interest. I wondered whether Emilia had visited out of curiosity while she was in the area, or whether she intended to take him away. I needed to know, so I settled Robert down with Julie and some toys and went to find Leah. She agreed to find out what Emilia's purpose had been in coming to the orphanage, and returned to say that, as far as the director knew, Emilia had come merely to visit Robert and see how he was getting on. She had stayed only a short while, and had left with no apparent emotion towards him. I hoped that Dr Popescu had recommended to Emilia that Robert be adopted, but I wasn't very optimistic.

Thanking Leah, I went back to Robert with a lighter heart, and stayed with him until afternoon sleep time. Just as I was preparing to leave, a message came to say that there was someone to see me at the front door. My first thought was 'Emilia! She's come back to demand money or threaten me or tell me that she is going to have Robert after all.' Trembling, I pushed through the heavy front door, and saw Mair smiling at me.

'Hi!' she said, 'We're going out into the countryside now for a bit, and thought you might like to come with us.' I practically fell into her arms in gratitude, and squeezed into the back of the car, thanking God for giving me these friends in my time of need. Hannah and Rebecca were giggling over the water situation, which had left John marooned in the shower that morning, and their teasing brought a welcome air of normality. The family were eager to know what had happened, and telling them about it helped me to cope with all the emotions involved.

We drove out into the mountains with the sun streaming down out of a bright blue sky. It was idyllically beautiful, with the light bringing a sharp definition to the panoramic views and mountainscapes. My heart ached for all those who couldn't enjoy such beauty and freedom, but I determined that I would not allow my feelings to spoil the pleasure we had in being together in these lovely surroundings. We stopped by a fast-running stream bordering a forest, and had a picnic. The girls rushed off to explore, and soon we were all involved in a game which required crossing the stream without getting wet and hiding in the forest. It was great fun, and the combination of sun, beauty, peace and friends was very soothing.

By the time we got back into the car and continued our drive, I was feeling greatly restored. After a spectacular tour through the mountains, we returned to Mihaela's apartment for a cup of tea, and then later in the evening all of us, including Mihaela and Adrian, went out for a meal. They were still feeling shy and didn't like the idea of letting others pay, but it was a lovely relaxing evening and provided a wonderful break from the stresses of the law courts, as well as a farewell to Mair, John and the children, who were going back to Bucharest the following morning.

The next day was 1st May, a public holiday in Romania. Mihaela and Adrian got up very early to go and work in their grandparents' village. Like many of the townspeople, they helped to tend the family smallholding when they could, despite having full-time jobs. Adrian owned a cow, which was kept in the village, and sold the milk to friends and neighbours. Visitors would frequently come to the flat with old Coca-Cola or lemonade bottles to fill with milk from the small churn Adrian brought back from the village on his bike. There was no concept of sterilising the bottles or pasteurising the milk, although Mihaela used to boil her own milk.

They had gone before I woke up, and I enjoyed a rare lie-in, taking the opportunity to catch up on lost sleep and restock my depleted energy reserves. I went down to the orphanage in time to play in the gradina for a while with Robert and the others and then to help with lunch and toileting. When the children were settled down for their afternoon rest, I went across the road to visit the Simu family. Only Alexandru was there; he told me that Rodica was returning to Romania on Sunday with Andrei. I was very pleased for them, but wished that I could say I was returning to England on Sunday with my son.

The days seemed to drag by as we waited for Wednesday and the adoption hearing, although I kept very busy. I spent a great deal of time in the orphanage, and also helped Mihaela as much as I could. Our friendship was deepening as time passed, and we really enjoyed time spent together. We went shopping, went to church meetings, had tea with Neli, Adrian's cousin, visited the translator and watched television. If it wasn't for the uncertainty over Robert, and my desire to return to the children and Graham, I would have enjoyed myself whole-heartedly. It was exciting and a privilege to be immersed in another culture, and I tried to make the most of the opportunity. I wanted to remember as much as possible to tell Robert about in later years, so that he might know his heritage and be proud of it.

During this time, I obtained permission to take Robert out of the orphanage to have a passport photo taken. Diana the educator was detailed to come with us, presumably to ensure that I didn't run off with Robert. There are no photo booths in Alba Iulia, so we went to a photographer, who sat Robert on a stool in the middle of the studio and flashed lights at him. Robert didn't like the experience and kept trying to escape, staggering towards the door while looking pathetically at me, as if to ask why I was allowing such things to happen to him.

There was some question over the passport which I didn't quite understand. It concerned his birth certificate, and seemed to involve returning to Cimpeni. I couldn't get a clear story and felt anxious: going to Cimpeni would mean another day in Alba, together with all the logistical problems of getting a car and driver to go there. But I had learnt patience, and decided to leave it to God – and Nicu – and not worry about it until it was an issue. More immediately, I was becoming increasingly concerned that the British Embassy had been right when they said that entry clearance to Britain was a requirement in court before an adoption could be legalised. I imagined everything else being in order, and then the adoption being refused because

I didn't have an entry visa. But it was too late now. The adoption hearing was the next day.

I woke up early, feeling even more nervous than last time. I didn't know what the day would hold, or what demands would be made on me. The uncertainty about Emilia continued, and I didn't feel that confident about Domnul Cornel either. But underlying all these natural fears and emotions was a deep unexplainable peace, a belief that the Lord would achieve what he had promised and that he was in control. This was no glib mantra, and did not prevent me feeling physically ill with nerves, but it was a fundamental reality in my consciousness. In spite of all that depended on the day ahead, I felt an amazing joy bubbling up inside me.

Adrian, Mihaela and I set off early for the Judecatorie, and again when we got there Emilia and Radu had not arrived. There was every likelihood that they would cut their losses and not bother, but I felt an assurance that they would come. To my relief, after about an hour I was proved right, and they came into the law courts, looking somewhat defensive. We waited nervously for Nicu, who told us that we would have to wait until 12 o'clock for Domnul Cornel to be available. Emilia and Radu obviously had a problem with this. Mihaela explained that the only bus back went soon after 12.00. As it was still only 9.30 a.m., they had understandably expected to get the business completed in the morning. I couldn't bear the thought of wasting another day, let alone of Emilia losing patience altogether and refusing to return a third time.

'Come on,' I said to Adrian, 'let's go and find Domnul Cornel and explain the situation ourselves. Perhaps he'll change his mind when he realises that Emilia can't stay.' Adrian looked very dubious and seemed about to demur, but I had already moved off, glad to have some action for my over-stretched nerves.

We walked round to the nearby Municipal Buildings and along endless corridors until we found the right office. Predictably, Domnul Cornel wasn't there. We waited outside the door for what seemed an age. I was getting more and more impatient, so eventually Adrian went off in search of him, and came back after a short while with the Municipal Prefect in tow. He gave me an insincere smile, and I tried to explain the problem, helped out by Adrian. After some debate, which Adrian handled, Domnul Cornel nodded decisively and gathered up some papers and a file.

'What's happening?' I whispered – my most frequent question.

'He's coming to the court with us *now*,' Adrian whispered back. I was startled at how easily the Prefect had changed his plans, and hurried along before he changed them again.

When we got back to the law courts there was no sign of Emilia and Radu. My heart sank. Surely they hadn't given up already? While I was scanning the main hallway for them, Nicu disappeared. Within a few minutes, Domnul Cornel had also gone. I felt as if I was in the middle of some Agatha Christie novel, and half expected to hear blood-curdling screams from an upper room. Tense with frustration I went outside, and there, among the many groups of people apparently conducting business on the street, were Adrian and Radu standing together. Emilia stood a little apart from them, her shoulders bowed but her face as impassive as ever. Radu was shouting, his face dark with anger. I knew that he was still demanding money, and I felt fearful. I edged closer, unnoticed by the protagonists, but Emilia saw me and an enigmatic expression crossed her face. It was impossible to tell whether she liked me or loathed me. I could only catch snippets of the dialogue, but I didn't like what I did hear.

Suddenly, I felt as if I couldn't handle the situation a moment longer. A little boy's life was being haggled over, and all that I had fought for was slipping away. I started crying, and sobbed out in broken Romanian, 'I don't have lots of money, and I don't want to break the law. I only want to help Robert and make him happy. I love him.'

With that, I broke down completely, and Adrian put his arm round me. To my astonishment, Emilia was crying as well. She came up to me, and we hugged each other, sharing for a brief moment the indefinable infinite emotions of motherhood. Then she took my hand and said, '*Hai!*' Hand in hand, we went up the steps into the Judecatorie, and up to Nicu's office. Amazingly, he was there, and so was Domnul Cornel. We were actually ready for the adoption hearing at last.

We were taken into an anteroom, and then Domnul Cornel was called through into an inner room. After a short time he came out, nodded a curt farewell to the rest of us and went away. A lady came out and asked us to go in.

It was not a conventional courtroom, with jury seats and a place for the judge and defendants, but it was quite large and arranged in a formal manner. There were seats set out on either side of a central aisle, and at the front was a large table, behind which sat two men and a woman. The usher showed me to one side and Emilia to the other, and then went to sit at a side table covered in files and papers. Nicu took up a position near the front, on the same side as me. At a word from one of the judges, he began to speak, putting the case for the adoption of Robert.

After a while, the same judge turned to me and asked a question, which Nicu translated, concerning Robert's handicap and our ability to help him in it. I answered in English, but put some words in Romanian, to the evident approval of the panel of judges. Encouraged by this, I answered their other questions – about how we came to be adopting a Romanian child and how long we had been involved with Robert – with as much Romanian as I could muster. Nicu added to my answers, often referring to the documents in our file, of which the panel had copies. They seemed interested in our other children and surprised that we wanted another.

Then they turned their attention to Emilia. I strained to understand what was going on, all the while marvelling at the fact that I was actually standing in a Romanian court, alongside Robert's natural mother, pleading my case to adopt him. The experience had a dream-like quality, yet in it all I was very much aware of the presence of God, upholding me and guiding my words.

Eventually, after some sharp questioning, the judge asked Emilia if she gave her consent to us adopting Robert. There was a fractional pause. I held my breath, wondering if, even now, she would refuse or run out of the room again. She turned her head and looked into my eyes.

'*Da*,' she said, almost inaudibly, and moved forward to sign her name. I breathed a sigh of relief. At last she had done it. She wouldn't have the chance to change her mind again. I was asked to sign as well, to confirm my intention to adopt and care for Robert Sanducan Toldea.

One of the panel summed up the case, and then we were motioned to go. But what was the outcome? Was Robert now our adopted son under Romanian law? Nicu told me that technically it was still not assured. The panel of judges would issue a decision based on the hearing, and only when I was in possession of a signed sealed and stamped adoption decree would I be Robert's legal parent.

'But will they agree to the adoption?' I asked, upset to discover that it was still not over.

'I think, yes,' said Nicu, smiling. 'It is just formalities now.' But I didn't allow myself to celebrate too much yet. God had promised and he would do it, but the Romanian authorities might still have some delaying tactics up their sleeves.

I went downstairs, still trembling from the ordeal of the 'trial', as the Romanians called it, and went to see if I could find the others. Mihaela, Adrian, Emilia and Radu were all standing together, looking uncomfortable. There was no obvious emotion on Emilia's face, and I reminded myself that she had seen Robert only a couple of times in all his life, and had never made any attempt to get him back. Perhaps any guilt she had about that would be assuaged now, as she allowed him the opportunity to be part of a family. We all shook hands formally, and I gave Emilia some presents for her children. It was a strange moment. Impulsively, I gave her a hug by way of farewell, feeling that curious affinity with her again. She smiled and turned away and we watched them go, relieved that our dealings with them were over, and yet sad for them as well.

My days of waiting in the Judecatorie were apparently not yet over. We went back in and sat outside Nicu's office while he sorted out the various courses of action we would have to take. There were other documents to obtain: a new birth certificate, a passport, something for the police (though I wasn't sure what) and, of course, the entry visa for Britain. To my relief this hadn't been mentioned during the adoption hearing. The British authorities required Emilia's social report and the medical before they would issue entry clearance, and these still had to be translated into English. We sat on a bench near Nicu's office, squashed up against lots of others waiting to see their lawyers.

Eventually Nicu emerged from his office with some papers. We had to take one set to the secretaries' office on the third floor and one to the passport office in the town centre. Before we went, Nicu drew Mihaela to one side, talking to her seriously but not urgently. She looked rather uncomfortable. As we walked towards the passport office, she cleared her throat nervously a few times.

'The er . . . lady who takes writing in the court . . .'

'Clerk?' I supplied.

'Yes, the clerk to the court. She . . . er . . . wants a present.' I was puzzled.

'Present? What for?'

'To type out the adoption order. She say it will take two months to type.' I was horrified.

'Two *months*? But an adoption order won't be much more

than a few sides of A4!' Then light began to dawn. 'How long would it take if she had a "present"?'

Mihaela looked more uncomfortable than ever. 'Two days.'

I was seized by an almost uncontrollable fury. How dare this woman bribe us like this? After all we had been through, to be held to ransom at the last minute.

'This is outrageous!' I shouted. 'I can't believe she would do such a thing. We must report her to her superior.'

Mihaela shrugged. 'It would not do any good. Probably her superior would want some of the present too. This is Romania. It is normal.'

I remembered Rodica saying something very similar, and realised that there was really very little I could do to challenge the system. It seemed that the economy of the country relied on bribery and corruption at every level of society, to the extent that it was considered part and parcel of everyday life. So I had to choose between giving her a present for doing her job, or holding out on principle – and waiting two months before I could get Robert out of the orphanage. It was insupportable.

'What about Nicu?' I asked. 'Can't he do something to help?'

Mihaela shook her head. 'He is very sorry, and not pleased, but he dare not say anything, in case they do not give us the adoption papers at all.'

I realised that, once more, I would have to rely on his judgment. If I made an issue of this I risked jeopardising the whole proceedings. I couldn't rely on the clerk backing down if I were to confront her. Maybe I was just being weak, exhausted by the traumas of the past few weeks, but I didn't feel like fighting this one.

'OK,' I said, resignation in my voice. 'What would be appropriate?'

Mihaela spread her hands expressively. 'Oh, coffee, soaps, chocolates . . . it does not matter really.'

'I have some perfume at home. Would that be all right?' I

had brought many gifts with me, to use as genuine thank-you presents. It galled me to use one for bribery. Mihaela nodded.

'Perhaps. We will see.'

The perfume was a reasonably expensive bottle of eau de toilette, extremely expensive in Romanian terms, but when Mihaela saw it she gave it the thumbs down. 'No, it will not do.'

'Why ever not?' I asked, quite put out. 'It cost a lot of money.'

'But it is too little,' said Mihaela apologetically. So the size of the present was more important than its value. I learnt that many larger items of comparatively little worth were acceptable in the bribery stakes, whereas one small but valuable item was not. What a strange system, I pondered, intrigued despite my irritation. I would have to consult Mihaela when it came to giving Nicu a thank-you gift. He had never asked for money or a present, and had made it clear that he was paid by the state and needed nothing more. I had always believed his motives to be genuine, and wanted to show our appreciation of all his work and effort on our behalf.

The next day, we went back to the Judecatorie bearing our bag of goodies: coffee, a bar of chocolate, some toothbrushes. I also had some clothes and food for Robert, in the hope that we would be able to get him out of the orphanage that day. We went up to the clerk's office. I stayed outside while Mihaela went in with the bag. I was too squeamish – and too annoyed – to do the actual deed. Mihaela came out soon, and told me in a whisper that Carolina, the clerk, had been very pleased with her presents, which had been slid unobtrusively under the table. The adoption order would be ready for the next day.

I felt very disappointed that it would not be available today. Somehow, I had expected to release Robert almost immediately. Each additional delay seemed harder to bear. Then Mihaela gave me the news that Domnul Cornel also required a present for his part in the proceedings. I was beyond speech!

This man was an official of the civic government, a public servant. He had merely been doing his duty – and had taken a very long time about it – in compiling a report on Emilia. Mihaela said that he had allegedly caught a cold and sore throat as a result of his expedition to Horea, and thought that a present would be some recompense. I snorted in disgust, and then picked up on a vital difference between his demand and Carolina's. Domnul Cornel had finished his work, and it had been filed at court. There was nothing he could do about it if I refused his corrupt request.

Mihaela looked a bit upset at this suggestion. 'Yes, for you it would be all right,' she said, 'but we are still here, and he could make things difficult for us if we should ever do business in the courts or at the government centre. Also, he would be angry with Nicu.' I hadn't thought of this: of course, Mihaela and Adrian and Nicu were associated with me, and my actions could adversely affect them after I was safely back in Britain. It was a sobering thought.

'OK,' I sighed. 'What would dear Domnul Cornel like as a present?' She smiled in relief and suggested whisky or brandy. I realised that I didn't have enough presents, if I were to keep to my original plan of giving gifts to those I really wanted to thank, so I went off on a tour of the shops to see what they would yield. There were certainly more imported goods available than even a few months previously, but they weren't usually of very good quality. The prices were low for a Westerner but high for someone operating only in *lei*, the Romanian currency. Inflation was escalating, and lei were buying less and less. I found some things I hoped would be suitable and took them home for Mihaela's scrutiny.

I also had more official business to do. Now that the adoption was virtually complete, I needed to hurry along the British side of things and obtain an entry visa for Robert. I was aware that my plane ticket was due to expire the following week, and I wanted everything in order before then. The visa was still awaiting some sort of validation from the Home Office and the translations of the medical and social reports. I rang Daniela to see if they were ready, but she had not quite finished. This was frustrating: I had discovered a fax machine at the post office, but it closed down, for some mysterious reason, at 3.00 p.m., so I would have to collect the translations later and try to fax them very early the next morning. Knowing how unreliable the phone system was, I didn't hold out much hope for the fax machine. I collected Robert's passport photographs – a pale wasted face with huge eyes staring out from under the shaved head – and went to pay some tax into the court. That done, there wasn't really much more I could do to hasten events. As ever, I was learning patience the hard way!

The next day, Friday 8th May 1992, I was up early and down to the town. To my amazement, it took no more than half an hour to get the fax through to the British Embassy, although I had great trouble phoning them to say I had sent one! I went round to the law courts and waited for Mihaela and Nicu to arrive. Together, we went upstairs for the Adoption Decree, that precious piece of paper that meant a new life for Robert and a changed one for the rest of the family. Carolina, the clerk, was ingratiatingly friendly. Her smiles made me feel faintly nauseous. She presented the two sheets of A4 paper with a flourish, as if she had accomplished something incredible. She also mentioned that Madame Presidente, one of the chief judges, who had been at the hearing, would like to meet Robert. Clutching the decree as if my life depended on it, I left the room, hardly able to believe that at last the miracle had occurred. Robert was legally our son! We still had to get him a new birth certificate, but Nicu suggested that we fetch him first, so we hurried over to the Casa de Copii, bursting with impatience to snatch him away from that dreadful place.

10

La revedere, Romania

He was in the gradina, with other children from his dormitory and the English aid workers. They were delighted that we had finally succeeded in our quest, and helped me to change him out of the orphanage clothes and into the shorts and shirt which I had bought specially for him. He hated being changed; it needed two of us to get the job done! That achieved, I carried him inside to see Dr Popescu. She was unusually friendly, and actually smiled and wished us well. I signed a form releasing Robert from the care of the orphanage, shook her hand and walked out. I could hear the shrieks and cries of the other children, and my heart ached for all those left behind. If I could have taken them all, I would have done.

As we closed the heavy gate behind us, both Mihaela and I were in tears. It was a very moving moment. Robert was free, and our tears were of joy, as well as grief for all the suffering he and his peers had experienced.

'You're my little boy now,' I whispered to him. 'You're part of the family.' He stared solemnly at me, then smiled, not understanding my words but responding to the love underlying them. We skipped across the road to Rodica's house, wanting to share the wonder of the occasion. Unfortunately, neither she nor Alexandru were at home, so we introduced Robert to Domnul and Domna Simu and then went on to the town hall. I was still carrying Robert, as his walking was very unsteady and slow, but he was so light that it was no effort.

At the town hall, the ladies in the birth certificate department made a real fuss of Robert and promised to issue a new certificate for him *imediat*. He sat on my knee as we waited, watching them seriously, and every now and then reaching out to touch something on the table. I kept giving him a hug, as if to remind myself that he really was there. His hair and skin were suffused with the smell of the orphanage, and I vowed to bath him as soon as possible. Soon we had a new birth certificate for Robert Sanducan Smith, and it occurred to me that, somehow, Nicu had worked it so that there was no need to go to Cimpeni again after all. I would be able to get Robert's passport in Bucharest, and then collect the entry visa.

All I really wanted to do was get on a plane to England and be with Graham and the children again, but there were so many tasks still to complete. Yet they didn't have the same power to frustrate and annoy any more, not now that I had Robert safely with me. The delays and obstacles were over at last. No matter what happened now, he was our son, in law as well as in faith. Every now and then, I burst into thanks to God for having kept his word and achieved the impossible.

Back at the Judecatorie, I felt as if I was walking on air. How many hours had I spent here, waiting, uncertain, disappointed? Now I had Robert in my arms, the culmination of all the agonising and effort. It was a moment of triumph, unnoticed by anyone except Mihaela and me. We went up to Carolina's office. After exclaiming effusively over him, she accompanied us up to see Madame Presidente. The judge was genuinely interested in Robert, and asked intelligent questions about his condition and possible development. She laughed when Robert tried to catch the large bow at her neck, and held his hand before we left, wishing us well in the future. Her attitude was a welcome contrast to other officials we had dealt with, and helped to restore a balance after my recent experiences with Carolina and Domnul Cornel.

We caught sight of Nicu as we passed his office, but he was in a rush and only able to stay a few minutes. He spoke kindly to Robert and stroked his head before preparing to move off. I tried to thank him for all that he had done, but the time and setting were not appropriate. He brushed aside my thanks and bowed in farewell as he hurried away. I didn't want that to be the last I saw of him, and decided that I would call round to say goodbye and thank you properly before I left Alba Iulia.

We took a taxi back to Mihaela's apartment. Robert was very subdued and withdrawn, and stood stiffly in the middle of the flat while I found him some of the baby food I had brought with me, knowing he still couldn't chew. He ate the whole jar and some pudding, but without enthusiasm; I managed to get him to drink some milk as well. I remembered how distressed Ionela had been about feeding, and was grateful that Robert didn't seem to have a similar problem. In the hope of encouraging him to chew, I offered him some of the chocolate that Emilia had given him when she visited, but he wasn't interested and merely clutched it in his hand until it started to melt.

Normally he would have had a sleep about this time, and he was looking very tired. I was a great advocate of afternoon sleeps (with three pre-school children, they were essential — for the mother rather than the children), but I had to take the adoption decree round to Daniela's for translation into English as soon as possible. Robert would just have to forgo the sleep and go to bed earlier that evening. I got out the pushchair I had borrowed and strapped him into it, wondering if he would object. But he seemed to like it, and made one of his rare sounds as I began to push. It was definitely a gurgle of pleasure. My heart lifted at the sound. Life was going to improve from now on for Robert Sanducan Smith.

The last few days in Alba Iulia passed quickly. Robert was fearful of many aspects of life that we take for granted. He slept on the sofa bed with me, and went off to sleep immediately each night. When I woke in the mornings, it was to see a dark pair of eyes staring at me. As soon as I made a move, he scrambled up and clung on to me, terrified of this new unknown environment. He was also frightened of being undressed and of having his nappy changed. The first few times

I bathed him, although I tried to make it as much fun and as unthreatening as possible, he screamed throughout, gripped by panic yet not making any move to escape or struggle. Even simple things, like moving from one room to another or preparing a meal, were fraught with fear for him. He shied away from any sudden movement or noise, and for much of the time remained still and vacant, his mind unable to take in any more new experiences.

Yet I was beginning to see changes in him already. He started to take more interest in the toys I had brought, examining and experimenting with them rather than merely clutching on to them. He smiled and even laughed more easily, and began to communicate with Mihaela and Adrian as well as with me. At first, it was not much more than eye contact – a look at us to see what we were doing or how we were reacting, or a smile as we looked at him – then he progressed to touching or pulling at us to show us what he wanted. They were small beginnings, but they gave me great hope.

Robert continued to like the pushchair, which was just as well as I still had tasks to complete before I left Alba Iulia. He greeted its unfolding with great excitement, and would try and sit in it before it was ready. While he was in it, he didn't seem frightened of traffic noise or crowds of people, and would sit there quite happily as we went on various journeys: to the passport office, to Daniela's, to the travel office in an unsuccessful quest for train tickets and to Nicu's house, to say thank you.

I had thought long and hard about how to express my appreciation for all that Nicu had done for us. I didn't want it to seem as if I was giving him a 'present' of the Domnul Cornel type. Nicu had never asked for money or a present and had always acted with the utmost integrity, and I didn't want to insult him. Yet neither did I want to leave without showing due thanks. It was a delicate problem, and I consulted Mihaela about it. She seemed a little uncertain herself, which surprised me. Evidently she was not accustomed to honest lawyers! In the end, we put together some gifts for the whole family, and I walked round to their apartment.

Nicu wasn't there but Elena, his wife, welcomed me in. She didn't speak English, so our conversation was limited. How could I possibly express all the gratitude I felt? I knew that without Nicu the adoption wouldn't have been possible. He was God's provision to us, but there was no way I could say all that in Romanian. I did my best, and Elena flushed in embarrassment when she realised that the bag I was carrying was for them. She kept shaking her head and saying that it was 'not necessary'. Robert sat in his pushchair and looked round the elegantly furnished apartment, his eyes attracted by the large pictures on the walls and the bright rugs scattered on the floor. In another room, watching television, were Nicu and Elena's two children, dark-haired dark-eyed boys of about five and seven, too shy to do more than peep round the door and then run off. I shook Elena's hand and made my farewells, sorry not to have seen Nicu one last time but glad to have discharged my burden of thanks. Elena smiled warmly at me and waved as I made my way down the stairway of the apartments, Robert under one arm and the pushchair under the other.

The next day, Sunday, was our last in Alba Iulia. Adrian was going to preach in one of the outlying villages, but Mihaela decided to stay behind. I was just feeding Robert his breakfast when the phone rang. I could tell from Mihaela's voice that it was someone she wasn't at ease with, but I was surprised when she handed me the phone.

'It is Nicu!' she whispered, 'He invite us to go out today!' I took the phone, not knowing what to think. Sure enough, Nicu was inviting us to join his family to go 'by mountains'. He had spoken before of their pleasure in walking in the mountains, and had said that he would like to take me out there, but I had assumed he was merely being polite.

I explained that I was with Mihaela, and he said that the

invitation included her as well. When I put the phone down to discuss the matter with her, Mihaela looked flustered and unsure.

'No, no, I will not go,' she said. 'You go, but I must stay here for when Adrian returns.'

'We could leave him a letter,' I suggested, 'telling him where we've gone.' But she obviously felt very uncomfortable at the thought of spending a day with the lawyer and his family, and was not to be persuaded. I was in something of a quandary: I was touched by Nicu's invitation, recognising it as his way of responding to the gifts we had given him, and did not want to insult him by refusing. I was also keen to see some more of the country while I had the opportunity, but I didn't want to hurt Mihaela by going out on my last day. I tried to explain all this to her, aware that Nicu was hanging on at the other end of the phone.

'You go,' she insisted. 'That is OK.' Feeling that it was indeed the right thing to accept the invitation, I spoke to Nicu and arranged to be picked up within the next half hour.

Nicu was the proud owner of a Skoda, apparently quite a status symbol in Romania. We all squashed in and chugged along through the flat hinterland surrounding Alba Iulia, heading towards the mountains. Robert sat quietly on my knee, uneasy but not too frightened by this new turn of events. Not for the first time, I wondered how he would react to the plane journey.

After we had been travelling for about an hour, we stopped in a small village and turned into the yard of a single-storey whitewashed house with the characteristic steep roof shape of rural Romania.

Nicu turned to me and smiled. 'The house of my parents,' he explained. 'We visit them.' Everyone got out of the car, glad to stretch their legs, and Nicu's boys dashed into the house, shouting with delight to see their grandparents.

I felt quite shy but was put at ease by the warmth of the

welcome we received. We were ushered into the best room, where Nicu's mother brought in some soup for us. I still couldn't get used to the variable mealtimes in Romania. Sometimes there were enormous gaps between meals, so that I would be ravenously hungry, while at other times, as now, two meals followed each other in quick succession. However, I was moved by the hospitality offered and ate with smiles of thanks.

Everyone made a fuss of Robert but he sat solemnly next to me, not moving or making a sound. Afterwards, I coaxed him for a little walk outside, and we looked at the pig in its pen and the hens wandering around the yard. There was a long strip of land planted with vegetables and fruit trees, at the end of which was the toilet, a shack containing a hole in the ground. It made me realise again what a soft Westerner I really was. These rural homesteads looked so attractive, with their connotations of a more simple and purer way of life, but would I really want the poor sanitation and the arduous labour involved in completing the most basic of domestic tasks? Numerous Romanians felt the same, which was why so many of the villages were diminishing in population as young people moved to the comparative luxury of the towns and cities.

We had been joined by Nicu's sister, Magda, and her two young children. After some time chatting with the grandparents, during which I played with the children in the yard, we set off again, this time for the monastery of Rimets. Our first glimpse was through the trees: pale, almost Mediterranean buildings, with decorative roofs and brickwork, nestling against the mountainside. It was still a working monastery, with dormitories, a refectory and workshops as well as a large church, dark and heavily ornate in the traditional Orthodox style. I shivered as I gazed at the baroque paintings and detailed mournful statues. Aesthetically the building was beautiful, whether the style was to your taste or not, but spiritually there was an air of foreboding, even menace. Maybe I was allowing my ever-active imagination to run away with me again, but I was glad to return to the sunny courtyard and visit the workshops, where the monks still weave rugs and blankets using traditional looms. There were some beautiful pieces of work, vivid and intricately patterned, destined, I suspected, for the tourist trade. I was tempted by one in particular, but even with the good exchange rate it was quite expensive, and anyway far too bulky to carry along with a child, pushchair and luggage. One day, perhaps, I would come back for it . . .

Robert, meanwhile, had been sitting in his pushchair, apparently quite happy to take in the experience from this safe haven. He made very little sound and occasionally tapped his head and closed his eyes. I had noticed, however, that the head-tapping was becoming less frequent since he had left the orphanage, and I hoped that it would soon stop altogether. We had a picnic lunch by a stream, and the other children ran around enjoying their freedom and paddling in the shallow water. Robert sat and watched, but made no effort to follow them. I prayed that one day he too might run and paddle and laugh, free to be truly a child.

Nicu was keen to go further up the river. It seemed that the mountains became even more stunning there and the river very dramatic, with beautiful falls and interesting rock formations. We parked where the track petered out, and continued along a path by the river. He was right. The scenery was amazing, and I was overawed by the beauty around me, seen at its best with bright sun, blue skies and blossom on many of the trees. After a while, the path became too difficult for young children, with lots of clambering over rocks and steep banks. Elena and Magda volunteered to look after all the children while Nicu and I continued a little further to where the path ended at some falls. I hesitated at leaving Robert, feeling the responsibility of looking after him was mine alone, but realised that I was being irrational: I knew he wouldn't mind being left, particularly if he was in the pushchair. Although he recognised me now, the bonding wasn't deep on his side. Any adult who showed him attention and kindness was acceptable to him.

Promising to be as quick as possible, we climbed and clambered and at one point even waded our way towards the falls. It was a challenging walk, appropriate, I thought, for my last day in Transylvania. I would take away happy memories of an exciting, beautiful, but not easy time. The waterfall was worth the effort. The river burst with tremendous power through weirdly shaped rock formations, and roared its way down the steep hillside. We were in a canyon, with the mountains rearing up above us at close range. Nicu smiled at me and spread his hands expressively, as if he had some personal part in producing this spectacle. He saw the delight and awe on my face, as I struggled to give vent to my reactions. It was hard enough to articulate in English, let alone Romanian. He laughed understandingly, and I gave up and enjoyed the beauty in silence as we slowly made our way back to the others.

It was early evening by the time we arrived in Alba Iulia again. We had stopped at Nicu's parents' for a meal, which was very welcome but made us later than I had envisaged. It had been a wonderful outing, though, and I was glad that I had accepted Nicu and Elena's invitation. After all the traumas and problems, it had been good to have a relaxing happy day with no black cloud of uncertainty hanging over me. It had been good to spend time with Nicu and his family as friends, away from the formality of the lawyer–client relationship. I was very grateful to them for their kindness in taking me out, and extremely surprised, therefore, when they presented me with gifts as I got out of the car. I protested but they insisted, saying that they wanted me to take away something to remind me of them and my stay in Romania. I gave them a farewell embrace, feeling quite emotional, and stood with Robert by the roadside to wave as they drove away.

Mihaela and Adrian seemed quite agitated by how late it was and said that they had been worried about us. I apologised profusely, explained the situation and showed them the gifts that the family had given me, including some still-warm pastries from Nicu's mother. I felt sorry that Mihaela and Adrian were upset on our last evening together, and wondered what I could do to improve things. Whatever decision I had made today, I would have upset or offended someone. I suddenly felt exhausted by the constant effort of trying to discover the right way to behave in an unknown culture, and couldn't wait to get home, where it came a bit more naturally!

Eventually, though, we had a very pleasant evening together, chatting, reminiscing and laughing over the events of the past few weeks. As the time came to leave for the station, we all realised how emotional we were about this parting, for we had become such good friends, bonded by our faith and the intense experiences we had shared. We prayed together before we left, and I felt moved to pray particularly that they might have a child. I was sure that the Lord wanted them to be parents, and I asked him to make it possible. Mihaela and Adrian had been married for seven years and had been trying to conceive for some time. I knew this was a great grief to them, and I prayed that as they had given themselves to rescuing Robert, God would give them a child too. We were all in tears at the finish.

Several times in the previous week, I had tried to buy train tickets for the sleeper, but without success, so we went straight to the ticket booth on arriving at the station.

'*Nu!*' The girl in the ticket office couldn't have been less helpful.

'Oh, surely she must have some sleeping compartments?' I protested. 'Tell her I have a young child. I don't mind sharing a berth with him.' Adrian tried again, while the queue in the noisy draughty booking hall got longer. I was still feeling emotional at the thought of saying goodbye to Mihaela and Adrian, and the prospect of having to sit up all night with a fidgety, perhaps terrified, child was too awful to contemplate. Adrian came away with a shrug of defeat and two first-class tickets. There was nothing for it but to sit up all night and hope that we could doze a bit.

I was travelling down with Jenny and Alex, two workers from Project Alba, and they had also failed to get sleepers. I swallowed my irritation and dismay, for these were my last moments with Mihaela and Adrian and I didn't want them spoiled. As the huge train pulled in and people scurried to find their compartment, we kept beginning sentences and then not knowing how to finish them. Saying goodbye is always difficult, but infinitely more so when you don't know when, or if, you are going to see each other again. With Robert on my hip, I leaned out of the train window, thanking them again for all they had done, promising to write and send photographs, vowing to come back. Mihaela was crying, and they both began to run along the platform as the train moved off, waving and calling goodbye until I lost sight of them in the inky darkness.

Robert clung on to me, disliking the strangeness and the noise of the train. I settled him down on the seat, pulling it into a lying position, as people do on the overnight train. This really only works if the compartment is half full. Any more than three and there is nowhere to put your legs! There were six in this compartment, but by sitting opposite Robert and sharing the two seats I hoped to make the journey as comfortable as possible. Unfortunately this hope was not realised, and I spent the night trying to find a suitable position to doze, listening to the customary loud debates that always seem to accompany Romanian train journeys and keeping an anxious eye on Robert. He lay still most of the time but didn't sleep very much. Instead, he gazed at the ceiling, vacant and unmoving, as he had done for so much of his young life. I was sorry to see this reversion, but also relieved that he did not fidget or whine all night.

By the time we got into Gara de Nord, we were all aching and heavy-headed. Helped by Jenny and Alex, I gathered all my stuff together, put Robert in the pushchair and went off in search of a taxi. Mair and John had visitors from England. While this wouldn't normally have stopped them giving me a bed for the night, these particular visitors had recently failed yet again in their attempts to adopt a child, though not one from Romania. Mair, feeling that it would be insensitive to give a great deal of attention to Robert and me, had arranged for us to stay with Ruth, the lady who had come with us to see King Mihai. I invited Jenny and Alex to come back to her flat with me for coffee and a wash, knowing that she wouldn't mind in the least. Among aid workers 'in the field' there is a great deal of mutual support and casual hospitality. People know that they can be sure of a welcome and understanding whenever they need it. I was right, for Ruth greeted us all warmly and made us breakfast. I felt a tremendous urge to lie down and go to sleep, but couldn't give into it: a marathon trek round various Bucharest bureaucracies awaited me.

Ruth offered to come with me, for which I was very grateful. I didn't really know where to start in this vast city, and trying to do things with a small child in tow was far harder than when there was only me to consider. Armed with the pushchair, several jars of baby food and a spoon, nappies and Ruth's map of Bucharest, we hailed a taxi and careered off to the police headquarters (population department). After a long wait there, we were told to pay some sort of tax and come back the next day. So we hailed another taxi and went right across town again to the passport office. It took ages just to find the right room in this rambling building, which seemed to consist mostly of corridors, opening out occasionally into ill-lit ill-signed rooms. We were sent backwards and forwards; when we eventually arrived at the correct room for my admittedly unusual but not unique requirements, it was time for Ruth to go to work. She was doing an afternoon stint at the street children's shelter, then would come home for a few hours before working through the night. I wondered whether I would still be in the passport office when she began her night shift.

We waited hours. Occasionally, someone would ask me a question and my hopes would rise, but then nothing would come of it and I would sit for another age until another question was asked. At last, an official came back and told me that the passport would be ready in a week. A *week*! Even after all this time in Romania, I still couldn't believe my ears. It was all too much to bear. I began to explain the urgency of my situation, and as I did so my voice began to wobble and I started crying. The official looked horrified, and with a muttered '*Un moment!*' he disappeared. Still upset, I sat and cuddled Robert, oblivious to the curious stares of the others who were patiently waiting. To my surprise, the official returned in a few minutes. Brandishing some documents at me, he said tersely, '*Reveniti miine*' – come back tomorrow! Breathing a prayer of thanks I left, pondering the power of tears. I hadn't intended to cry, but it had proved very effective. My next stop was the British Embassy, within walking distance, and I hoped that I would not be provoked to tears there, whether unintentional or otherwise.

The sentry looked a little askance at me as I pushed the buggy through the checkpoint. Wasn't he used to children coming here, I wondered, or did he think I had taken a wrong turning on the way to the kindergarten? We went through the security doors and waited while Ms Hitchens was called. Robert chose this moment to make some of his rare sounds, and the high-pitched squeaks reverberated round the stately rooms. I smiled placatingly as people's heads shot out of office doors, and wished Ms Hitchens would hurry up. When she did come, she looked surprised and not pleased to see Robert.

'This is most unorthodox,' she said in a severe tone. 'You shouldn't have adopted him until you had entry clearance from Britain.' No 'Congratulations!' or 'Isn't he lovely? I'm so glad for you both.'

'The court didn't require it, so I wasn't going to raise the subject. I can prove that he is legally adopted, and all I need now is entry clearance so that we can go home.'

'What about a passport? We can't grant a visa without that.'

My heart sinking, I replied, 'It will be ready tomorrow. But couldn't you at least ring Britain to check that everything is ready?' Some of the documents required for entry clearance had not reached the Home Office when I had last enquired. If she rang today and authorised it, everything would be complete when I brought the passport in the next day. But she wasn't going to co-operate.

'No. I must see the passport first. And then we should really wait for the originals of the documents to be posted out here.' Frustrated, I tried to explain that I needed to get home, my ticket expired in two days' time, my other children hadn't seen me for a month . . . It was no use; she was immovable and I left, feeling utterly dejected that, in the end, it was the British who had made things so difficult for me. Somehow, I had expected more warmth and fellow feeling from them, as if, likening the whole experience to a battle, they ought to have been on my side, and weren't. Exhausted, I trailed back to Ruth's flat, and after some food fell asleep next to Robert.

The next day, the weather had changed quite dramatically. Dark clouds glowered in a leaden sky, and every now and then came the ominous rumble of thunder. It was still very hot, almost oppressively so. I had arranged to visit the Pughs on my way to or from the Embassy and passport office. I also had to go back to the police headquarters having paid the requisite tax, but that would have to wait. I wasn't sure why I had to go back, anyway.

Just as I got to the Pughs' it started to rain, and I was glad to get inside before it got any worse. It was marvellous to see them. Their visitors were out, so we had coffee and a chat. They were delighted to see Robert and remarked on his progress in the week since they had last seen him. It was encouragement I needed to hear. Mair glanced out of the window.

'Why don't you leave him here for his sleep while you go to the passport office and the Embassy?' she suggested. 'It's stopped raining now, but it looks as if it'll start again soon, and you haven't got a cover for the buggy.'

What about your friends?' I asked, doubtfully.

'Oh, they won't mind,' she assured me. 'They're pleased for you, really. And he'll be asleep for quite a while, I should think.' Robert did look very tired, and I would be able to complete the business much more quickly without him.

'OK. Thanks. I'll be as quick as I can.' With that, I was out of the door and away, hurrying towards the passport office.

I got there just as the rain was beginning to come down heavily again, and I dashed into the nearest entrance. A man barred my way. Puzzled, I said *'Scuza-ma!'* and tried to get past. But he shook his head and shouted something I didn't understand. What was going on? All I wanted was to collect Robert's passport and get to the Embassy. I attempted an explanation, but he didn't try to listen and I started to get angry. Abruptly, before I lost my temper and got myself arrested, I turned round and walked into the rain, at a loss to know what to do. 'Lord, please help me. I feel at the end of my tether,' I prayed, remembering (a little late) that I was not without resources.

At that moment, I spotted someone coming out of a side door further down the building. There was no one else around because of the downpour, so I slipped in and found myself quite close to the room I needed. Business seemed to be progressing as usual; obviously the place was not closed. The incident with the man at the entrance would probably always be one of life's little mysteries. I showed my documents to the girl at the desk, and after a comparatively short time a man appeared, holding the precious book. There it was, a Romanian passport, with Robert's lost little face staring out from it. For although he was legally my son under Romanian law, he was not a British citizen, and so had to travel with his own passport and the special entry visa to allow him to come into the United Kingdom. I felt like throwing my arms round the man, but contented myself with thanking him with a warm smile and leaving swiftly.

I was greeted with a crash of thunder as I came furtively out of the side door. The skies opened and the rain sheeted down. Within a minute, I was soaked to the skin, with water dripping off every part of me. There was no point in taking shelter, even if I had time to, so I battled on. The rain was coming down so quickly that it was almost solid, and the wind was blowing it against me, actually causing pain as it battered my bare skin. I was extremely glad that I didn't have Robert with me. By the time I passed the Anglican church where I had worshipped a few weeks back, the water on the street was nearly ankle deep and horribly dirty. I had to wade past the building, because a drain had blocked and there was no way round. I thought about all the vital documents in my bag, and prayed that they would not be badly damaged.

Well might the sentry at the British Embassy look askance at me this time. I must have looked like the proverbial drowned rat! I dripped through the distinguished portals and stood awkwardly in the elegant hall, a puddle of dirty water forming on the polished parquet floor. The air conditioning, normally very welcome, made me feel cold, and after announcing my presence I squelched over to the Ladies, uncomfortably aware of how closely my skimpy summer clothes were sticking to me.

At length, Ms Hitchens came clicking down the corridor, looking cool and fresh. I gave her the passport, hoping to hear that the visa was just the formality of a stamp. But no. Apparently the Home Office had not yet sent over the documents required for entry clearance to be granted.

Couldn't you ask for them to be faxed, please?' I pleaded. 'I *have* to fly tomorrow. I've complied with all the regulations, and haven't tried to take any short cuts. It's imperative I have the visa now, and I'm prepared to wait.' She gave me a long considering look, perhaps hearing the underlying desperation in my voice. Or perhaps she didn't want this bedraggled, grimy British subject in her elegant embassy any longer than was necessary.

'Well, maybe, in the circumstances of you already having the child . . .' she said. 'I'll telephone the Home Office. Please wait here.' She walked smartly off, and I waited. Time ticked by, and I thought idly that if I were a mathematician I could employ myself by working out what proportion of my time in Romania had been spent waiting: in offices, law courts, railway stations, shops, airports, the Embassy . . . Surely, after all this, I thought hopefully, I'll never be an impatient person again.

A secretary popped her head out of a nearby room. Perhaps she was going to offer me a cup of coffee.

'We wait for a phone call from the UK,' she said, '*Imediat.*' She disappeared again, leaving me resigned to a long wait. I had never known *imediat* be used literally; it always seemed to indicate some unspecified time in the future. Maybe it was the Romanian equivalent of *manyana*. At last, Ms Hitchens returned, carrying a file. She was smiling.

'I have faxes of all the documents required,' she said, 'and have completed entry clearance for Robert.' She handed me the passport, duly stamped, and a form for me to sign. I could have kissed her!

'Right, everything is in order now, so it only remains for me to wish you all the best with your new child.' I thanked her and we shook hands in true British fashion. I nearly danced out into the street, such was my relief at having completed all the formalities. Now all I needed to do was confirm my flight home, and book a ticket for Robert.

11

Welcome to the family!

The rain had stopped and the sun was once again piercing the remaining clouds, making the streets shine as the pale light reflected on the water. The city looked fresh and clean after the storm, although there were now quantities of mud and debris on the pavements, swept into soggy piles by the onslaught of rainwater. Workers and shoppers darted to tram stops and the underground, glad of the respite to make their way home. I splashed back to Mair's apartment, looking forward to a bath and a change of clothes.

Robert was still asleep when I arrived, even though it was nearly teatime. All the unaccustomed stimulation and attention had worn him out. After the welcome bath, I had a cup of tea with the family and recounted the events of the afternoon. I remembered that I still hadn't returned to the police headquarters. John looked at the forms that I had been given there and the proof that I had paid some tax, and suggested that I post them back, rather than going there in person. This seemed an excellent idea, especially as Mair offered to post them for me. (I was still no wiser as to what the forms were in aid of.) Now I had nothing left to do in Romania except leave.

I rang the Tarom office to confirm my flight and request a place for Robert. Although he was only two, it was still necessary for him to be allocated a separate seat. To my dismay, I discovered that there were no spare seats on the flight. Mine was booked, but obviously Robert's wasn't yet, and the staff would not take a booking. They said that since they couldn't guarantee a seat for him they would not issue a ticket. After all the rushing and persuading others to speed up procedures, it looked as though I wouldn't get home the next day after all.

John was experienced in Tarom's working practices and tried to calm me.

'Let's go down there,' he said. 'They always say there are no seats, but often they have cancellations.' We dashed to the car and sped downtown; it was twenty to six, and the office shut at six. I knew that the assistants would stop work on the dot, even if they were halfway through some business.

We were shuttled from one counter to another. Finally we found someone who would deal with us. 'You can buy a ticket anyway, but there is the danger that there won't be a seat for him,' she said. I agreed to buy it. I really couldn't believe that the flight was completely full, and even if it was, surely they would accept a small child when his mother had a booked seat. He could sit on my knee for the whole journey if necessary.

It was five to six, and the girl discovered that her credit card machine didn't work. We had to join another queue for the payment to be processed. I was on tenterhooks in case the clerks downed tools before I got my ticket. Right to the end, this adventure was characterised by uncertainty. We raced back to the girl who had been dealing with us, and she handed me the ticket. It was six o'clock.

'I'm sure there will be a place for him on the flight,' John said reassuringly as we walked back to the car. I could only hope that he was right. Any delay now would be costly in money, time and my own well-being. Physically, mentally and emotionally, I was exhausted. I needed to get home.

The next day I woke early, before Robert. I looked at him, his dark eyelashes moving slightly on his pale face, his mouth slightly open as he breathed, and I was overwhelmed with tenderness for him. He looked so vulnerable, and he had so many painful memories to eradicate, so much damage to be repaired. All being well, by the end of the day he would have joined his new family and could start his new life. Our hope was that then healing and wholeness would begin.

We had the apartment to ourselves as Ruth was already at

the shelter. She wouldn't be back before we left, so I wrote a little note to accompany some small thank-you gifts. After breakfast, impeded by Robert, who kept walking off with anything I picked up, I gathered together all our belongings and packed them, leaving out anything that might be required on the journey. Robert would need to be fed and kept amused in a restricted space for at least three hours. I was not looking forward to it.

I had arranged to be taken to the airport by Vanu, a taxi driver who had regular work with the Pughs. It seemed strange to be leaving in such a low-key manner, when it was the climax of all that we had worked towards. After a year of struggles and reverses, I was taking Robert home. Surely there should be cheering crowds to witness such triumph and joy! Instead, I locked the empty apartment behind me, and, unnoticed, got into the taxi and left the city. Gazing out at the dirty streets and the ugly concrete apartment blocks, I remembered vividly my first view of them all those months ago. We had no idea then what the future held. We were ignorant of Romania and its people. We didn't know who was going to be our child, nor how long and how difficult it would be to get him. All we had was an unswerving belief that God had sent us to rescue a child in distress. So much had occurred since then. Now, at last, what we had struggled for and believed in had finally been accomplished. I had our adopted son on my knee, and we were going home to England.

At the airport, I shook hands with the kindly Vanu and went into the checking-in area, heaving along in stages my heavy luggage and Robert in his pushchair. It was an anxious moment when I checked in. Would they reject Robert's ticket and tell me to come back for a different flight? I held my breath as the girl glanced at the tickets and passports, filled in a form and then dealt with the luggage. She handed me two boarding cards and transferred her attention to the next passengers. We were on! Yet not until we were actually in our seats and the plane was moving did I allow myself to believe that we both really were leaving Romania. I held my thin, frail child close, and thanked God for keeping his promise.

Robert didn't like the plane and was very restless. I had given him some Phenergan, as my GP had suggested, to calm him during the journey, but so far it didn't seem to be having any effect. As the plane took off, I cuddled him and covered his ears. I disliked the sensation myself, and couldn't imagine how it would feel to someone who until recently had never been outside the walls of the orphanage. He whimpered, but didn't scream as I had feared he might. Looking down at the landscape beneath, I realised afresh how much I loved Romania, despite all the dreadful things I had witnessed and experienced there.

'We'll come back one day,' I whispered to Robert. 'You'll be proud of your heritage.' He squirmed and fidgeted on my knee, uninterested in the view or his heritage. I tried toys, but they lasted for only a few minutes. All I wanted to do was sleep but as Robert obviously didn't I had to stay awake. The Phenergan seemed to have made him more active than usual rather than making him sleepy, and he constantly crawled over me or the seats or along the aisle. He was in a world of his own and, try as I might, I couldn't seem to get through to him.

A lady sitting near by came and sat next to me. (There were actually quite a few empty seats on the plane.)

'Excuse me, but I just wondered. Your little boy, is he one of the Romanian orphans?'

I nodded, and she began to ask all about him and his adoption. She was a kind person, genuinely caring, and I didn't object to her questions. But my emotions were still too raw to be able to talk with equanimity about all that had happened. Several times, I felt myself near to tears and was glad of the distraction of Robert's restlessness.

The plane began to lose height, and Robert started to moan and cry. He was weary and confused, and he didn't like the feeling in his ears. I cuddled him and tried to divert him, revitalised by the thought that we were nearly there. As the plane touched down, relief and joy finally overwhelmed me as we arrived back in Britain at last.

The airport formalities took longer than usual. I had to go through passport control twice, once as a British citizen, and then back through a different channel for Robert. The passport controller, as unsmiling as they all seem to be, examined his passport for a long time, looking at each page carefully and asking questions concerning the adoption. I began to wonder, with dread in my heart, whether something was wrong with the passport or entry clearance. Then he stamped it and said, 'Adoption visa, valid for one year,' and we were through. I collected a trolley (no porters guarding them jealously here) and Robert sat on the top, looking around him with huge eyes. I kept up a stream of talk to him, but he didn't really respond. It was all so strange for him, but he seemed more overawed than frightened. Even when I moved away a little to pick up some of my luggage from the carousel, he did not appear upset. There was so much vying for his attention, all assaulting his under-stimulated senses at once. No wonder he couldn't respond. The luggage all appeared, and I piled it on and walked wearily through the customs area. My next task, I thought to myself, was to get to King's Cross for the journey back to York. But I was wrong.

'Mummy, Mummy! We're here!' Four little boys flung themselves on me, laughing and shouting and crying. It was one of the most wonderful moments of my life. Having greeted me, they crowded round Robert, kissing and talking to him. Strong arms held me close, and Graham hugged me as if he never wanted to let me go.

'We're home!' I said, smiling through my tears. 'The family is together again at last.'

The children were wildly excited to see me again and to meet their new brother for the first time. We put him in the pushchair, and I leaned on Graham and watched as they offered Robert toys and told him their names. They held his hands and stroked his shaved head. His huge brown eyes stared at them, uncomprehending.

'We've got your cot ready for you,' said Joel.

'And your teddy,' added Barnaby. Simeon was dancing around in front of the pushchair, trying to make him laugh. But Robert was very solemn. He didn't look frightened, but obviously couldn't make out what was happening. He clutched the soft toy parrot that I had given him in Romania, and gently banged his head with it.

We moved towards the car park, with the older boys jostling for position to push the trolley and pushchair, and Graham and me trying to re-establish contact with each other. So much had happened, and we were both feeling so emotional that it was difficult to know what to say. We kept looking at each other in wonder, unable to believe that we were all actually together again. At last we had achieved our goal, and yet the expected exhilaration was not yet present. I was reminded of the feeling immediately after the birth of a baby. The agonies and sheer physical demands of labour leave only exhausted relief and discomfort. Only later does pure joy and euphoria come flooding in. It was the same now. We had to adjust to the fact that he really was here, and recover from all the pain and uncertainty of the previous weeks before we could truly feel and articulate the tremendous joy and elation deep within us.

Robert accepted the car seat without a fuss, to our relief. We were worried that he would be frightened. But then, I reflected, it was quite similar to his beloved pushchair, with the added advantage of being higher, so that he could see more. It was a long journey, and the other boys were quite restless. All their pent-up emotions concerning my absence and the advent of Robert were expressed in a noisy exuberance throughout the four and a half hours of travel. Each child was eager to tell me snippets of news, and ask me lots of questions about my own activities. I was so grateful to be back with them, although somewhat weary by the time we approached York.

On the way, we stopped for a picnic lunch, which Graham, working to heights of efficiency, had prepared before leaving that morning. We found a nice spot away from the motorway in a wood, and the boys rushed off to explore, charging through the undergrowth and climbing accessible trees. Robert stood there smiling, making happy noises which made me want to cry. I told myself that I was going to have to stop being so weepy! I was not normally someone who cried that easily, but the last year, and particularly the last month, had changed me.

We all sat down to eat, except Robert, whose attention was engaged by a large stick nearby. He picked it up and waved it in the air, attracting our attention with a loud whoop. His brothers laughed in delight, and shouted encouragement to him. He started to stagger around, shaking the stick and laughing out loud. It was a beautiful sound. The other boys, pleased with this evidence of Robert's happiness, got up and grabbed sticks as well. Within a few minutes, all five of them were running around like some primitive tribe, shouting and waving sticks in the air. Graham and I looked at each other and smiled, moved by love for our children and the resilience of their spirits.

There were crowds of people lining the street outside our house. When they caught sight of the car, they started to wave and cheer. Dumbstruck, I glanced at Graham, but he looked as bewildered as I did. The house was festooned with yellow paper flowers and ribbons, and over the front door was a large poster, proclaiming 'Welcome home Sue and Robert'. This display and the crowd of jubilant caring friends on the pavement was too much, and I began to cry again. Robert's story had affected the whole community in Poppleton, and they had turned out to welcome him home. I recognised people from the church as well, who had travelled across the city. It was so moving, and

I didn't know whether I could cope with it.

The children were thrilled at this reception and couldn't wait to get out of the car and join the party. Robert sat quietly in his car seat, looking vacantly into the distance. Graham lifted him out and carried him across the road to meet the well-wishers. I followed behind, too emotionally drained to do much more than hug people and say how glad I was to be home. Everyone was so pleased to see us. They crowded round Robert, smiling and talking to him, asking me questions and chatting to the other children. Robert didn't seem upset by the fuss that was being made of him. He stared intently around him, occasionally making a grab for an ear-ring or baseball cap. The smiles and laughter of the picnic were gone now, as he assimilated this new situation, but he was evidently not unhappy. Already, he had come quite a way from that withdrawn, uncommunicative child of the orphanage.

Eventually, we crossed back to our house again, and Graham put Robert down by the gate. Before we could catch up, he had walked on alone into the front garden. Behind us, the chatter died down as everyone stopped to watch him. Slowly he staggered in the direction of the front door, and then stopped and squatted down, his attention caught by a paper flower which had come loose. He examined it for a minute and then picked it up and held it out towards us, a smile on his face. Everyone breathed out an 'aahh' at this small gesture. Somehow it symbolised hope for the future.

That night, as we tucked him up in his cot with the teddy Val had given him lying by his side at last, we thanked God for keeping his word and achieving the impossible to rescue this little child from a desperate situation. The lessons of faith that we had learnt as we strove to adopt him would be needed just as much as we embarked on the huge task of bringing him up. We didn't know what damage he had sustained from all the deprivation and neglect, nor how he would develop from now on. Even if his alleged handicap did not have a specific medical diagnosis, he still had very many special needs, and it was impossible to tell how these would be manifested. There would probably be many times when we would need to remind ourselves that it was God who had called us to have Robert in our family and who had made it possible, and therefore it was God who would make it possible for us to deal wisely with him.

The first few days were rather strange, as we adjusted to the changes in our family and Robert learnt his way around. He spent quite a bit of time wandering from room to room, picking things up and putting them down again some time later. He always had something clutched in his hand, and he soon learnt that items could also be stored in pockets. Simeon, Joel, Barnaby and Nathanael were very kind to their new brother. They showed him all the toys and helped him to sit up for meals, talking to him all the time, as if he understood what they were saying. It was obvious that in their own way they had been very moved by Robert's plight, and wanted to make him happy. There was no sign of disturbance or jealousy from any of them, though we looked out for it with eagle eyes and worked to give them extra individual time so that they didn't feel left out. After about a week, it began to feel as if Robert had always been with us.

He couldn't walk properly, or talk at all. His food had to be liquidised and he was still in nappies. Severe malnourishment made his bones stick out, and his face was emaciated, with sunken eyes. He had worms and scabies. His awareness of life around him was still very limited, and he was terrified of normal activities such as bathing and hairbrushing. Undressing him for bed provoked screams, and when we first cut his hair and nails it took three of us to hold him down! Gradually, though, as his memories faded and he grew more accustomed to his new home, he ceased to object to these physical necessities.

He still preferred tactile experiences in his explorations, a throwback to the years when he had only the feel of the cot bars to stimulate him. He liked the feel of Stickle Bricks, and would carry a piece around with him all day, pausing every now and again to rub his fingers up and down it. Sometimes he would retreat into himself completely as he felt an object with an interesting texture. For a few minutes his eyes would glaze over and his tongue protrude as he gently stroked the surface. Once, when Graham was wearing shorts, Robert discovered the feel of his hairy legs, and sat rubbing them with a look of intense concentration.

This phase didn't last very long, as Robert's brain became more and more stimulated by all that he heard, saw and did in his new life. Another obsessive habit which soon disappeared was the head-tapping. Within a week of his arrival, Robert was tapping his head only rarely, and very soon he stopped altogether. He continued to fiddle with clothes or his hands or face, but gradually that too became less of a fixation.

He was fascinated by the rabbit and guinea pig, and spent quite a lot of time sitting by their run, his tongue sticking out, watching the animals nibbling the grass. He also liked the sand-pit and soon learnt about putting sand in the bucket. A major step forward was the day he played in the paddling pool, splashing in and out with his brothers, undeterred by the water on his face and his lack of clothes. Every day, he was smiling more and multiplying the number of sounds he made. All the signs were that he was increasingly happy in his new home.

At first, it was like having a baby again, but it was soon like having a young toddler as he began to observe and copy what his brothers were doing. He loved all the toys and began to learn how to play with them, and he revelled in the freedom of the house and garden. The pushchair was still a firm favourite, and he cheerfully smiled at all the people who came to make a fuss of him when he was out.

Meanwhile, I was not progressing so well. Within a fortnight of my return from Romania, I was in hospital with hepatitis, and after Christmas I was back with a worse bout which left me severely debilitated for months. Looking after five young children is hard enough work when you are in the peak of health, but is almost impossible after something as dreadful as hepatitis. During the crisis months of both illnesses, we were helped by Anny, a friend from Leeds, who came and lived with us and took over the running of the household with amazing competence. The children loved her, and she was extremely patient with Robert. To her must go much of the credit for his early rapid progress, for I was unable to do little more than cuddle him and allow him to lie in bed with me whenever he wanted to. When I first went into hospital, Anny brought the children to visit me after about a week. Robert didn't recognise me, turning back to Anny to be picked up. I burst into tears, overwhelmed with sorrow that I had lost that bond of affection so dearly formed through the difficult weeks in Romania.

The illness was a big pressure in our lives throughout many months, and reminded us again of the lessons of faith we had learnt while trying to adopt Robert. We had to choose to believe God's word to us and to rely on his help in difficult circumstances. The children coped well with Mummy being out of action for so long, and then being weak and weedy for even longer. There were some days when I didn't know how I was going to get through to the evening, and there were others when I felt so depressed that I wanted to go away and not come back. Thankfully, this phase didn't last too long, and I was supported through it by the love and care of Graham and my family and friends.

Despite the crisis and the many months when I was not functioning at full capacity, Robert continued to develop at an amazing pace. He began to understand what was being said to him and to obey simple instructions like 'come here', or 'sit down'. One day, when my mother was staying to help look after us, we had some of the delicious chocolate cake she had brought. I gave a small slice to Robert so that he didn't feel left out. He still couldn't chew, and used to walk round with finger food in his hand for ages. I glanced up to where he was sitting on the patio, and noticed that not only had he put the cake in his mouth, but he was actually eating it.

'Mum!' I shrieked, nearly causing her to drop her cup of tea, 'He's eating. Really eating! You *clever* boy!' He looked at me in wonderment and smiled a chocolatey smile. It was such a small thing, yet it had enormous significance, for we had wondered if he would ever be able to eat solid food. And with chewing, surely, would come the ability to speak.

All the normal milestones of childhood were major achievements for Robert, because there was no guarantee that he would ever attain them. The medical report from Romania, so difficult to obtain, had been disappointingly sparse in information. There was nothing to explain the label of 'retarded' and no medical history beyond a list of immunisations. He was monitored by the Child Development Centre at York District Hospital, and tested for all sorts of disabilities and potential diseases. Nothing specific was found, beyond a squint and some evidence of brain inflammation at an earlier point in his life. This could have been meningitis or concussion, but didn't necessarily denote permanent damage. Like the rest of us, the doctors and therapists could only wait and see, and help where they could. It was wonderful to have such enthusiastic support.

We went to the Children's Centre regularly for a variety of reasons. Sometimes it was for a general review with Dr Heggarty, one of Robert's favourite people. The paediatrician would play with him, tease him, swing him round, run up and down the corridor with him, show him his instruments and watch him drawing. Robert would have a marvellous time and never realised that he had undergone a complete examination! He had come to Britain with a terror of doctors, thanks to the brutal way he had been treated by them. Dr Heggarty, and our GP, Dr Jackson, soon changed all that.

Another favourite was Wendy, the orthoptist, who tested his eyes and worked to correct his rolling squint. Robert loved the pencil light with which she examined his eyes and the games she played to test his eyesight. He always remembered the routines from visit to visit. All staff at the Children's Centre were enormously patient, and made the whole process fun. Wendy told me that if the eye had not been corrected, it probably would have ceased functioning altogether eventually. Robert had to wear a patch for a few hours each day, but he didn't seem to mind much. It made him feel important, and he liked the little sticker that went on the eye patch. Over the months, the eye began to correct itself, until it was nearly normal again.

As soon as he came to live with us, Robert began to make more sounds than he had ever made in the orphanage. Perhaps it was easier for him to differentiate sounds in the calmer and more secure atmosphere of the family home. He copied the noises his brothers made (not all of them good!) and gradually started to form words. For a long time he could only articulate single words, and again we thought that perhaps he would only ever be able to speak in this very limited way. Then, just before Christmas, as we were finishing bath-time with Nathanael and Robert and the other three were playing in the bedroom, there was a commotion outside. A car, pulling a sleigh on a trailer, was coming slowly up the road, accompanied by carols and men with collecting-boxes. On the sleigh was a plump man in a red suit. The older children went wild. 'It's Father Christmas! It's Father Christmas!' they yelled, thundering down the stairs. 'Quick! Let's go and see him.' Grabbing a little one each, we followed them outside and smiled as Father Christmas gave them sweets and promised to come back later in the month if they were good.

Robert looked in amazement as this strange apparition passed. 'Far Chrissie gone!' he said, pointing down the road after him. We looked at each other in elation. He had just put three words together! We hugged him and told him how clever he was, and the other boys started up a triumphant chant of 'Far Chrissie gone! Far Chrissie gone!' There was no looking back after that in Robert's linguistic development. From two- and three-word clusters, he progressed to incomplete sentences and then to quite complex structures. He was given speech therapy, to help his pronunciation and to monitor his speech generally, which was a significant help. After a while, the problem was no longer encouraging Robert to speak but finding ways to make him listen.

As he was nurtured and encouraged, his real personality at last began to flower. He was endlessly curious and would fiddle and poke anything which interested him. We had expected him to be quite unhappy and frightened for some long time, but he proved to be a cheerful child who smiled and laughed a lot. Where he had once been so vacant, he was now vivacious and alert, greeting strangers and friends alike with a beaming smile and expecting them to join in with whatever he happened to be doing.

Like many children, he would whine and moan if he didn't get what he wanted. Sometimes distraction techniques worked well, and he would be cheerful within minutes. At other times, though, he wouldn't let go of an issue and persisted in trying to do something his way, even after it was obvious that he was not going to succeed. Despite this, however, he didn't display any disturbing behavioural symptoms. He developed a remarkable memory and was able to identify people, places and objects long after he had previously seen them. We had feared that he might not enjoy being with other children, since he had been so withdrawn in the orphanage, but he was very gregarious and not at all shy. He started at the local playgroup in Poppleton, and loved it. The helpers were marvellously patient with him, and he loved the constant activity and large choice of toys.

Playgroup was followed by nursery school, where Robert blossomed under the care of Mrs Dodgshon and Miss Innes. We had discovered that he needed very definite boundaries in every area of his life, and his teachers were excellent at providing these. They were strict, but loving and patient as well. We noticed that some people tolerated quite disobedient and anti-social behaviour from him, perhaps thinking that allowances should be made because of his background. However, when this happened he became more wild and demanding, which was ultimately not good for him or those he was with, whether at home or at school. So we would set boundaries for him, telling him in advance what was acceptable or not in a situation, and showing him he was wrong when he transgressed the boundaries, as he inevitably did. At home and at nursery he was treated as no different from his peers, and he thrived on it, learning fast what was required. When he first went to school, he used to interrupt constantly at story-time or assembly. Now he only does it occasionally, when he forgets himself!

Our dealings with bureaucracy were not over when we finally brought Robert back to England. Within a short time we were again assigned a social worker, this time to oversee the British adoption of our son. Britain does not recognise the validity of the Romanian adoption alone, and requires all adoptive parents to adopt their children under British law as well. This can only be done after a year, but does mean that the child is then recognised as a British citizen and is eligible for all British legal rights. Robert was also assigned a guardian ad litem, to safeguard his interests. There were more forms to fill in, documents to submit and court applications to make, but we didn't mind because at least now we had him with us. There was not that gnawing uncertainty any more. The adoption hearing was 19th July 1993, three days after his fourth birthday. I was nervous all of a sudden, in case something should go disastrously wrong, but in the event my fears were proved false.

The law courts were empty, with only a handful of people waiting or walking purposefully along corridors. The hearing began promptly and was presided over by a lady judge who was very warm, despite the formality of the situation. She was obviously moved by the whole story of Robert's life, and out of sincere interest asked more questions than were strictly necessary. After the legalities were complete, she called the children up to her and let them try on her wig, allowing us to take photographs of the moment. She sat Robert on her knee and gave him a cuddle before wishing us well and dismissing us all. The guardian said that she had never before been to such a lovely adoption!

He was no longer Romanian under law, but we wanted him to know and be proud of his Romanian legacy. We had brought back quite a few mementoes of Romania, including some lovely water-colours and china. The children also had books and knick-knacks and, of course, we had many photographs. Romania was frequently in our thinking and speaking, even when the memories began to fade a little. We considered it vital that Robert should realise that he was special because he came from Romania, and that he had a positive identity there, as well as his more painful history. I missed the country dreadfully, especially during the months of my illness. It was almost as if I had unresolved grief connected with it. I kept crying about all the children I had got to know in the orphanage, and longing to go back and see everybody again. I felt such a close bond with the country and the friends I had made, partly because I had gone through such an intense emotional and spiritual experience during my time there. We were for ever linked with Romania, part of its future as well as its past, and wanted Robert to be aware of this.

As part of our desire to maintain positive bonds with Romania, we had kept in touch with our friends there, and we were so pleased when we were able to save up enough money to invite Mihaela and Adrian to stay with us. At first, they were diffident at the thought, knowing that they would not be able to afford to come and not wanting to intrude on us, but we persuaded them, delighted to be able to return some of the hospitality they had extended to us. They came in July, after the usual bureaucratic wrangling over passports, visas and tickets, and stayed three weeks, one of which was with Elizabeth in Leeds. It was so wonderful to see them again. They were amazed at the difference in Robert after a year's absence and commented particularly on his speech and his liveliness. Mihaela had tears in her eyes. 'He is so happy now!' she said, giving him another hug.

It was fascinating showing Mihaela and Adrian around, and seeing our country and culture through an East European perspective. They enjoyed the sights of beautiful York and its surrounding countryside, but their true wonder and enjoyment was reserved for the shops and supermarkets. When they first walked into our local supermarket, they were overwhelmed by the vast space, filled with aisle upon aisle of amazing goods. They had never seen such an array of food and household items, and kept exclaiming at the huge variety available. Then they did some mental arithmetic, and were astounded at the comparison in prices. I thought that they might resent all this conspicuous affluence, so painfully different from their own everyday life, but they were delighted with everything. They explored each aisle with great thoroughness, admiring the packaging and commenting on new concepts, like ready-cooked meals or chocolate mousse. I followed behind, half amused, half guilty, but pleased that they were gaining so much enjoyment from the trip. (We had only popped in for some bread!)

I was a little anxious about taking Mihaela and Adrian to church, knowing how different it would be from their own services in Romania and fearing that they might feel offended by the expressiveness of the worship. I needn't have worried; they were profoundly moved by the whole experience and joined in as much as they could, although they didn't quite manage to dance! They loved the songs we sang, and Adrian talked about getting hold of the music so that he could teach them to the musicians back in Alba Iulia. The church gave them a royal welcome, which they also found moving. Once more, we were aware of how our faith bound us all together, despite cultural and language differences.

It seemed highly appropriate that this lovely couple were with us for the British adoption, since they had seen us through the Romanian one. They came with us to the court and were present for all the proceedings. Afterwards, when we went to McDonald's for a celebratory milkshake, Adrian commented on how much easier it had been to adopt Robert in Britain than in Romania. He was right, but I realised that I was glad to have experienced the Romanian side of it, even though it had been so hard. We had made some good friends, which would not have been the case if we had been able to fly in with all papers complete, meet our prospective child, attend an adoption hearing and then fly out again with our son. We had deepened our knowledge of God, ourselves and another culture through the whole experience. We would never be the same again because of all that had happened to us, but we saw that as a very positive thing: an enriching experience which was of eternal value.

12

A future and a hope

'Taxi? You want taxi?' I grinned, as I remembered the first time I had heard that question, nearly six years ago. So the taxi drivers were the same, whatever else might have changed in the country, pressing in like a pack of paparazzi eager to get a scoop. I was back in Romania. The snatches of language I had already heard and the glimpses of the countryside from the plane had caused my excitement to mount to an almost unbearable degree. It was not my country, yet I felt renewed just by being back, as if somehow I belonged there.

It was important to all of us that we maintained our contact with our friends in Romania. Besides our interest and concern in their welfare, we wanted to know how the country as a whole was progressing in its slow haul towards democracy and a modern market economy. We were aware that many of the abuses present under the old system were still operating, and that bribery and corruption continued to be endemic. And what was happening to the orphanages? Was the influence of the West in terms of child-care and hygiene having any effect? Were fewer children being abandoned now that Ceausescu was no longer enforcing a large family policy? Or did the fact that contraception was prohibitively expensive mean that large families were happening anyway? We tried to keep as informed as possible, reading articles or books and watching any television documentaries that might appear. And I felt a compelling urge to return there and see for myself.

I waved aside the first few taxi drivers and looked around me in amazement. Bucharest Airport was barely recognisable, with clean smart departure and arrival lounges and immaculate toilets! There was a fountain playing in the middle of the hall, and sharply dressed businessmen were milling around chatting with colleagues. The cafe was spotless, with appetising food and none of the usual birds flying overhead, dispensing their random largesse. It could have been any small international airport, no longer distinctively East European.

The change in outward appearances became more noticeable as my journey continued. On the surface, the country seemed to be doing very well. There was a huge increase in goods in the shops, and a much greater variety than ever before. Most Western brand names were available, and many companies from Europe, America and the Far East were setting up in the country, rather than just exporting there. Expensive and fashionable clothes could be seen on the streets, as well as Western and Japanese cars. New office blocks were being constructed and completed in the towns, and small shops were springing up in every road, converted from ground-floor apartments. Window-shopping appeared to be the new leisure activity, with people looking in amazement at the unfamiliar goods and their five- and six-figure prices.

Yet perhaps all was not as it seemed from this initial impression. At the Gara de Nord, after an unpleasant encounter with the lady in the ticket office who sold me a second-class ticket for the price of a first-class, I was surrounded by street children, attracted by my rucksack. They spent their days begging around the station and their nights in the heating vents underneath. Crazed by hunger, cold and drugs, their lives were filled with pain and unhappiness. I shuddered to think that Robert might have ended up as one of them, and shared out the chocolates and satsumas I had brought specially for them. Not much had changed for the better for these children. There were still charities such as Ruth's doing excellent work in the streets of Bucharest, but the numbers of children continued to increase, uncared for by any official authorities.

It was wonderful to see Mihaela and Adrian again. We greeted each other with shouts of joy and exchanged enthusiastic hugs, thrilled to be together again. Life had changed radically for them as well. To all our sorrow, they had not succeeded in conceiving a child and had begun to think about adoption, inspired by Robert. There was a stigma about adoption in Romania, and not many couples considered it as an option. However, that attitude too was beginning to change. Mihaela and Adrian had begun making enquiries, but nothing had come of it. Some of the committee considering their case had not approved of them because they were Christians, and blocked their application.

There had been silence for many months, and then one day, in the autumn of 1996, I received a letter from Mihaela, beginning, 'My dears, we are a family at last!' A photograph of two beautiful babies dropped out of the envelope. These were Timotei and Teodora, five-month-old twins from a Christian orphanage set up by a Western charity in Oradea, many miles from Alba Iulia. God had done another miracle! I had whooped with joy and excitement and phoned her immediately (*and* managed to get through). She had been tired but very happy. The children were doing well and putting on weight, having been quite seriously ill in the weeks following their birth. They were born three months prematurely to a woman who had wanted an abortion, but had left it too late.

Now I rushed into the small living-room, converted into a nursery, and gazed in wonder at the two little figures sleeping in their cots. They appeared much smaller than their age, but as they woke up and looked enquiringly at me, I realised that in other ways they were developing normally. They were bright and alert, with happy dispositions expressed in their ready smiles. Timotei was the bigger and chubbier of the two, with a huge appetite. He was placid, happy to remain in one place and let the world come to him. Teodora was quite the opposite. Tiny, and with the distinctive head shape of the premature baby, she hated eating and virtually had to be force-fed. Yet she was brimming with energy and could nearly crawl. Her hands and feet were always on the move, and she accompanied all she did with a variety of interesting sounds.

It seemed so appropriate that Adrian and Mihaela, having given themselves selflessly to help us rescue Robert, should be blessed with children in the same way. There are still so many youngsters living in institutions who desperately need families and homes, yet the prevailing attitude remains against adoption. Our hope is that Mihaela and Adrian will be among the vanguard of a change in outlook, so that the stigma will disappear and many more Romanians will decide to take these children into their homes and their hearts.

Like everyone else, Mihaela and Adrian were trying to adapt to the transformation occurring in Romania. They too worried about the price of food, but were helped by their faith to be positive and forward-looking. In true Romanian tradition, they made money as they could, with various enterprises. For a while, they became full-time self-employed tailors, and certainly had more than enough work. The paradox was that they could never earn sufficient money because inflation, surging to a high of 60 per cent, had overtaken earnings so rapidly. No one could afford to pay what the clothes were worth, and they would work for hours and hours for a pittance that hardly bought them anything. So Adrian went into partnership with a friend, wholesaling bananas and oranges to small shops and markets in their area. They borrowed a large amount of money from family and friends and sold their car in order to buy two second-hand vans from Germany.

Twice a week, Adrian and his partner make the six-hour journey to Bucharest to buy the fruit and then come straight back, catching a few hours' sleep in the vans on the way. The rest of the week is spent in delivering the goods to towns within a fifty-mile radius of Alba Iulia. It is exhausting work, and Adrian is away from home a great deal, but they are able to make more money this way than from tailoring. With two children to feed and clothe, they have no option but to make as much as they can, even though they realise that it puts other strains on the family. Mihaela is left alone in the apartment to look after the twins for a great deal of the time, and when Adrian does return they are too tired and busy to maintain their own relationship at the depth they would like.

We talked and talked, about the twins and the job and life in general. It was a relief for Mihaela to unburden herself to someone who was not directly involved in the problems of everyday existence in Romania.

Then she asked suddenly, 'But what about you? How is the family? And how is Robert?' I got out the photographs I had brought, and looked at the little face with its mischievous smile, staring at me out of dark eyes alight with pleasure. How could I, in a few words, capture how Robert is now?

Like Romania, Robert has much from the past which shapes the way he is today. Years of deprivation and cruelty cannot be remedied instantly, however hard we work towards it. The process of change, miraculous as it is, can be painful. Robert's ongoing rescue from the effects of his background might prove to be as difficult in different ways as the original rescue from the orphanage. Yet, just as we discovered new depths of richness and joy through our challenging Romanian adventure, so there has been much fruitfulness in our lives in the ensuing years. It has been a privilege and excitement to see how Robert has developed physically and mentally, especially when we think of what would have happened to him if he had remained in Romania.

He is happy and energetic, living life to the full. Of course, he experiences the griefs as well as the joys of childhood – playground squabbles, tellings off at home and school, occasionally unsympathetic brothers – but generally he accepts his lot cheerfully and embraces all the opportunities open to him. He enjoys ball games and riding his bike, and goes to a dance class every week. Academically, he is not yet up to the average standard of his peers, but he attends a mainstream school, Osbaldwick Primary, with three of his brothers, and relishes every moment. He has a quick mind and a genuine desire to participate in all he can. Unfortunately, he often gets involved in things which are nothing to do with him, and neglects the things he is supposed to be doing! But despite the mental and emotional difficulties, the persistence and attention-seeking, the refusal to be quiet and listen, there is a zest for life and an inherent optimism which overcome the problems and disarm the critic.

After the initial burst of development in the first months, when he learnt to understand, chew, speak and become more independent, progress has been much less noticeable. The milestones are of a more subtle nature, and it would be easy to overlook them in the busyness of family life. Robert no longer stands out as being tremendously different from any other child, although he is still young for his age; at seven, his play is that of a three- or four-year-old, with frequent changes of activity and minimal concentration. The closest he comes to imaginative play is in dressing up, the favourite outfit being his policeman's uniform. He spends ages trying on dressing-up clothes and wandering round the house in them. The clothes are an end in themselves, not the means to an end.

Whatever is going on in the household, Robert is there, eager to participate. He loves to join in family games and activities, but cannot yet sustain them, nor can he sit quietly and learn. He likes the idea of painting, craft, jigsaws or Lego, but can rarely last more than a few minutes without becoming bored or, worse, interfering in someone else's attempts. At school, he sometimes tries the patience of his teacher by spending as much time telling everyone else what to do as doing his own assignments! Yet he is not malicious or unkind and longs to please, with a charming predisposition to be friendly and helpful.

The task of assisting Robert to mature emotionally and behaviourally is inevitably a long slow one, and not without its problems. He demands attention loudly and persistently and he will invade anyone's space to do it. How could he behave otherwise after being totally neglected for three years? Understanding his behaviour does not, unfortunately, always make it any easier to deal with on a daily basis. He has not yet gained the ability to empathise, to consider others, and still sees everything only from his point of view. Thus, he rarely listens properly to anyone else because his mind is running along its own track, and he interrupts constantly with his thoughts and ideas.

He is so congenial and willing to please, but finds it hard to play with other children without trying to take over or interfere with their games. Inevitably, this sometimes leads to conflict and rejection among his peer group. He is actually happier playing with children younger than himself. Though glad that his argumentativeness indicates an active mind, we do find it somewhat wearing, as he often takes an opposite view in order to be contradictory. This is the conduct of a young toddler in the body and language of a seven-year-old, and as such is quite hard to handle. We do lose patience with him sometimes, even though we love him and understand the causes of his behaviour. Yet, despite our mistakes and the very real problems he has, Robert is making steady progress in this area. Many of the children in the orphanage were very aggressive, but Robert is not at all belligerent. He has the capacity to be most affectionate, and our hope and prayer is that he will learn more appropriate social behaviour as he matures and becomes less egocentric.

It was impossible to explain all this to Mihaela and Adrian as they exclaimed in delight over the photographs of the children in our new house and in America, visiting my sister Penny and family. We had moved from Poppleton nearly two years previously, driven by the need for a larger house in our price bracket.

'To think this Romanian orphan went to Disneyland!' said

Mihaela, wiping her eyes. 'It is amazing!' I nodded. It did seem an extreme contrast. Robert had been captivated, as had we all, by the Magic Kingdom, which we had initially only visited because Penny lived so close to it. With his brothers he had almost exploded with excitement and wonder, racing from one marvel to another in the hot sunshine.

'He looks so happy now, and so English!' added Adrian.

'Well, he *is* English,' I pointed out, 'but he's also Romanian. He knows where he comes from, and we hope to come back in the summer as a family so that all the children can experience for themselves the places and people that they've heard so much about.' Mihaela and Adrian were enthusiastic about the idea, though a little dismayed because they wanted to offer hospitality but did not have space in the apartment. I was quick to reassure them that the seven of us didn't intend to camp out in their living-room! We did feel, though, that an important element in helping Robert to come to terms with his past was continuing to maintain an active interest in the country. Romania must be a reality to Robert, not just a story.

He had often looked at the photographs of our various visits to Romania, and as he grew older he began to ask questions about them. He knew that he 'came out of Emilia's tummy', and that there was a time when he was not part of this family. If he saw an item concerning Romania on the television, he was quite proud of the fact that he came from there, even though the article would inevitably present a negative aspect. Once he saw pictures of children in rows of cots and commented matter-of-factly, 'I was in those cots, wasn't I?' He didn't express any sadness about it because he could not consciously remember his time in the orphanage. His knowledge was theoretical and made him feel quite important, because he was now in a place of security and his only conscious memories were of his family and friends in England.

Robert had residual memories of Romania, but nothing that he could articulate. Instead, the scars were manifested in his constant need for attention, his short concentration span, his at times inappropriate friendliness and talkativeness. One day, he may be sad and confused about his background as he searches for his own identity in adolescence, and Graham and I must prepare ourselves for that, although we are not sure how. But as God has helped us and is helping us through all the other challenges of caring for our fifth son, so he will guide us in the right way through the minefield of the adopted teenager's agonies of growing up.

During my stay, I visited all my old haunts in the town and all the friends I had made: Rodica and Alexandru, Neli, and Nicu and his family. It was wonderful to see them all again and to re-establish contact that had been sustained by letter and cards. There was a real warmth of relationship which survived time and distance.

The tension of transition was evident wherever I went. Chatting to these friends, gleaning items from the news bulletins and making my own observations, I discovered that there were many paradoxes in the emerging modern state of Romania. Many of the changes were merely cosmetic, touching the external appearance but not reaching the heart. For the vast majority of people life was still very hard, and many were sinking into poverty, if not already submerged in it. Inflation was rampant, with prices rising weekly, yet with little or no commensurate rise in salaries. Most people could not afford the new goods which were in the shops. It was painful and frustrating for them to see the tempting arrays of foods, domestic equipment and electronic hardware but to know that they would never be able to obtain them. For a minority, entrepreneurs and those in high places in government, life had improved dramatically, but for the rest, the stark reality was that the price of bread had increased more than a hundredfold while their wages had hardly increased at all. It was impossible for people to look beyond the fundamental problem of feeding themselves and their families. The fact that circumstances should improve gradually meant little to them. Nor did their new-found freedom of speech, belief and movement cause great rejoicing any more. Life was too difficult to allow the luxury of philosophising.

Many people viewed emigration as the only way to improve their lot, and were investigating the requirements of any country that would consider them. Romania is not in the European Union, and so Romanians cannot work or live freely in Western Europe. Germany, with its welcoming immigration policy, had been a favourite destination, but with the problems of unification even Germany has had to tighten up. Canada, though stringent in its requirements, was allowing Romanians to become residents, and those who had gone, such as Adrian's brother Simion and family, sent back glowing reports of an affluent lifestyle with plenty for all. The climate and distance from family were disadvantages, though, and many of the emigrés planned to stay until they could become naturalised Canadians and then take the opportunity to live in Europe again. The prospect of a better life seemed no nearer in Romania, despite the outward signs of increasing prosperity. There was an atmosphere of discontent and frustration which coloured thinking and conversation and denied the possibility that conditions might improve eventually.

Rodica and Alexandru had flourished despite the bleak economic and political situation. Andrei, their little boy, had made marvellous progress and proved wrong all the authorities who had prophesied disability and handicap for him. He was an intelligent lively handsome boy, talkative and cheerful, making the most of being an only child and grandchild. Rodica and Alexandru finally managed to obtain their own apartment, but Andrei still spent a great deal of time at his grandparents' house, as his parents both went out to work. As a dentist, Rodica was able to earn a reasonable amount, but not enough to pay a nurse; she had to do everything herself, resulting in long hours. Alexandru continued to work for the German charity, delivering and monitoring aid into local orphanages. His hours were also long, but to some extent could be flexible to fit round Rodica's shifts. As always, they took an intelligent interest in what was happening in the country, and were always a good source of information and opinion.

Rodica's parents, Domnul and Domna Simu, continued their kindly hard-working lives much as before, attending church, tending the land and extending hospitality to many. They delighted in Andrei, and still held out hopes that Dorin, their son, would eventually marry and provide them with other grandchildren. Dorin himself was noncommittal on the subject!

Mihaela and I went to see the lawyer's family one evening. Nicu came to the flat to pick us up and took us to their new house. Of all the people I had met on my visit, he was the one who appeared to be doing best out of the changes in the country. Yet he was still the same gentle unassuming man that he had always been, notwithstanding his evident intelligence and ambition. He and Elena were now working as private lawyers in offices away from the law courts. He told me that they had more than enough clients, and were always very busy. I was glad that he was succeeding, because he was a man of integrity in a world which was still tainted with corruption. Their new house was enormous, but only a quarter finished! As we arrived, I thought that it was only a building site, but then noticed a light shining from a basement-level window. The family were living in the four or five rooms which were completed; the rest would be finished over the next two years. Their living accommodation was beautiful, with a high standard of building and decoration and some lovely design features. Mihaela's eyes were wide with wonder as we were shown round. She had never seen anything quite like it.

We met Dan, their older son, who was fluent in German and competent in English. He had been at a German boarding school in the town of Sibiu, where his younger brother now attended. At ten, Dan had changed to a school in Alba, so that he could focus on his English. I thought how lovely it would be if he and his brother could meet our boys in the summer.

One morning, with some trepidation, Mihaela and I went to the Casa de Copii in Alba, Robert's old orphanage. I pushed the gate open, and all the memories, never far from the surface of my mind, came flooding over me. I wondered how different it would be inside, if at all. The pungent smell was as strong as ever as we walked through the open front door and stood a little uncertainly in the entrance hall. A smartly dressed woman with a bouffant hairstyle came out of the office and enquired if she could help us. Mihaela explained our presence, and after a little discussion we were ushered into the reception room, where I had sat so often in the past.

'Dr Popescu has left,' whispered Mihaela. 'There is a man here now.' At that moment, a tall man in his thirties, with brown hair and deep blue eyes, came through from an inner office. He smiled and shook hands, asking many questions about Robert. He seemed genuinely interested in his progress, and made a few notes as we talked. What a contrast to Dr Popescu! He told us that he would be delighted to meet Robert if we were to visit Romania, and was pleased to receive some photographs of him, putting them carefully into a filing cabinet.

'Would you like to look round the orphanage now?' he asked. We nodded, smiling our thanks. It would be fascinating to see it once more, although the familiar feelings of dread were churning my stomach again.

The process of change in the country was reflected in the orphanage. The walls had more murals, and there were extra toys and clothes available for the children. New laundries had been installed, which made life easier for the staff and cleaner for the children. But the playroom, where once children ran wild in their free play time, was now filled with cots to cater for additional inmates, with only a small space for the dining tables. The orphanage was still grossly undermanned, with only a couple of staff to each salon of twenty to thirty children –

staff who even yet did not understand the basic concepts of child-care. The children continued to be confined to their cots for a great deal of the day, and remained uncontrollable when they were out of them. All over the country, training was taking place in the areas of nursing, hygiene and child development, but metamorphosis was painfully slow. The principles were in place but progress could only be very gradual, requiring as it did a whole revolution in cultural attitudes.

The orphanage was as upsetting as ever, but I was glad to have gone back, even though briefly. The staff remembered me, and were astonished at photographs of Robert. Most of his peers in Salon 2 had gone, sent on at three years old to other institutions, but there seemed to be no lack of children to take their places. Robert would have been sent to a home for the mentally handicapped, where, neglected and written off, he would have deteriorated rapidly. Without love, without care, without stimulation, he would have had no chance of development at all, physically, mentally or emotionally. If he had survived to eighteen, he would have been sent to an old people's home, or else been left to make his own way in the world, without home, money or support. The scenario is horrific, yet it has been, and continues to be, the fate of thousands of children in Romania and other similar countries.

I couldn't bear to think about what had happened to all those children I had played with and cared for during my previous visits to Romania and, instead, deliberately turned my thoughts to those I knew had escaped to a happier life. The Pugh family had left Bucharest a few years before and had returned to England. To our joy, they were living only an hour and a half's journey away, in Nottinghamshire, and we were able to continue our friendship at closer quarters. They had, with a few 'hiccups', finally completed Ionela's adoption, and the whole family, after an inevitable period of adjustment, had settled well into their new life. John still returned to Romania at intervals to lecture and train nurses throughout the country.

His reform package included aggressive privatisation, the liberalisation of almost all state-controlled prices and the abolition of foreign exchange controls and import quotas. With the support of the International Monetary Fund and the World Bank, the government believed it would be able to fulfil its promise to bring Romania eventually into stability and prosperity and an equal footing with its European neighbours. At grass roots level, people seemed to trust the promises, and faith in the country, mixed with a healthy realism, was at last being restored.

As I flew back to England, my mind whirled with all that I had seen and heard. Romania, in all its beauty and its bleakness, its fury and its friendship, was a part of our life as a family. We could not forget, nor did we want to, that the people, with their bitter past and uncertain future, were intertwined with our own destiny. God had brought us together, and maybe it was for more than the rescue of this one child.

Robert had been an 'irrecuperable', destined for the mental asylum and an early death. Now, five years later, he is living evidence of the flaws in the medical and child-care systems. The change in Robert from the gaunt, vacant, frightened little boy who first entered our home in May 1992 is, as Dr Heggarty, our paediatrician at York Hospital, said, 'nothing short of miraculous'. It was a miracle that we managed to rescue Robert in the first place, but since then we have watched and been part of a second miracle: the emerging of a normal, happy child from the straitjacket of deprivation and neglect. The pain of transition is always intense, and for Robert and for Romania the wounds are deep, caused by the suffering of the past. Healing cannot be instant, as there are so many areas which need restoration. Yet for both the country and the child there is a future and a hope.

Epilogue

The pale light of early morning reveals a small form snuggled in bed. His breathing is regular and his sleep-flushed face peaceful. Next to him lies a well-worn teddy, and various books are scattered on the floor of the cosy little room. His favourite toy of the moment is perched on his desk, and his clothes for the day are laid out ready on the chair. Gradually, the seven-year-old boy stirs and opens his dark eyes. He sits up at once, immediately awake and alert, pushing back his duvet and sliding out of bed. Another exciting day is about to begin.

He goes to the toilet and then pads into his parents' room. They are still in bed and he climbs in for a cuddle, telling them that he loves them. They respond sleepily, and he lies down for a few minutes, enjoying the warmth and security of being with them. Then he is off again, pausing before getting dressed to see if his brothers are awake. Distracted by a complex Lego model, he goes back to his room only when shouted at by the model's creator. Chattering loudly to another brother, he gets dressed and then bounds downstairs for breakfast.

He eats enthusiastically, talking all the while, interrupting the other children and taking no notice of their requests for him to be quiet. But they tolerate him, laughing at some of the things he says and ignoring some of the rest. He helps to clear away afterwards, and goes back upstairs to get ready for school, looking forward to seeing his friends and teacher again. He hugs Daddy goodbye and sits on the bottom stair and waits, looking at his reading book or shouting to the others, until Mummy is ready to take them to school. Life is rich and happy for the fifth child in the Smith family.

Helping Romania's orphanage children back into family life

Since the revolution, children in Romania continue to be abandoned, primarily because of poverty. Many families simply cannot afford to feed and clothe their children, and today there are 91,000 children living in the orphanages, of whom 8,000 are under the age of three.

The Romanian Orphanage Trust is the main UK children's charity working in Romania. The Trust believes that children belong in families and is working with the Romanian administration to keep vulnerable families together and, ultimately, to end the orphanage system. Over 3,000 orphanage children have already been reunited with their families by the Trust's British-trained social workers.

The Romanian Government is committed to reforming its child care system. Child care legislation is being redrafted and funding made available for new community-based services. The first orphanage is being transformed into a centre for child and family support services, including a mother and baby unit and a day care centre. Local adoption and fostering services are expanding to cover the whole country.

Further financial support is still urgently required to support this work. To a poor Romanian family a care parcel can mean the difference between bringing children home or leaving them in an orphanage. Each parcel costs just £25 and typically contains flour, sugar, potatoes, cooking and heating oil, children's clothing, nappies and a small cash grant.

For further information or to make a donation please write to or phone: The Romanian Orphanage Trust, FREEPOST SL2163, Slough, SL1 4BR; Tel: 0171 248 2424.